THE
Quilting Arts®
IDEA BOOK

EDITED BY VIVIKA HANSEN DENEGRE

the Quilting company

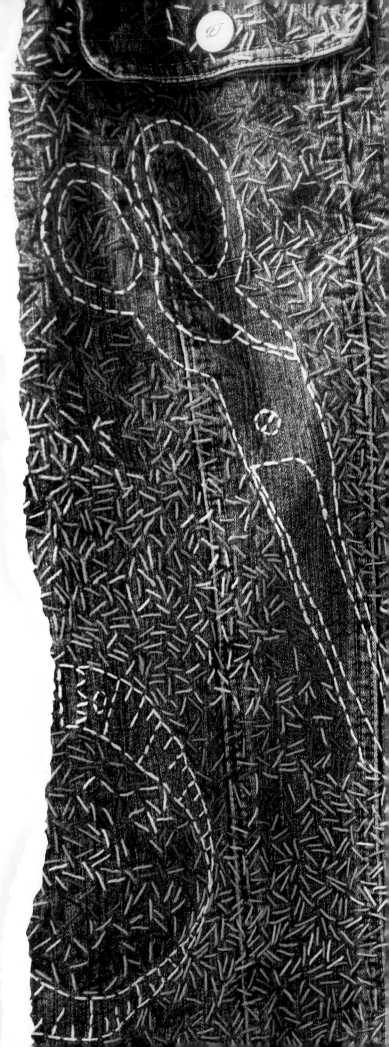

www.fwcommunity.com   www.quiltingcompany.com

22 21 20 19 18   5 4 3 2 1

SRN: R8573

ISBN-13: 978-1-4402-4884-9

EDITORIAL DIRECTOR
Kerry Bogert

EDITOR
Vivika Hansen DeNegre

CONTENT EDITOR
Jodi Butler

ART DIRECTOR & COVER DESIGNER
Ashlee Wadeson

INTERIOR DESIGNER
Pamela Uhlenkamp

PHOTOGRAPHERS
Larry Stein, Sharon White, and
Hornick Rivlin Studios

CONTENTS

THE
idea book

INTRODUCTION

There is not a day that goes by that I don't thank my lucky stars that I am surrounded by beautiful art made by beautiful people. And leafing through the pages of this book just solidifies that sentiment—I am fortunate, indeed.

All of the artists featured in this book have two things in common: they are passionate about their craft and open to new ideas. Without exception, every one of them knows their specialty like the back of their hand, but they are also willing to expand their skillset and try something new. Lynn Krawczyk constantly experiments with color and texture. Leslie Tucker Jenison challenges herself by working with paper as well as fabric. Jane LaFazio is always combining machine and hand stitching in new ways. And who would have thought of making tiny art quilts out of tea bags? Libby Williamson, that's who!

As an avid art quilter and the editor of *Quilting Arts Magazine*, I love learning from these artists and am in awe of what they do. Nobody does it better: from dyeing fabric and experimenting with unique substrates, to hand stitching and creating bold imagery, they are the best-of-the-best.

While you devour the beautiful photographs and the myriad of techniques in this book, I hope your curiosity is piqued and you use some of these great ideas in your own art. I encourage you to leave nothing behind: If art quilts are your passion and your creative expression is revealed through fabric and thread, then go make some art!

And if you're looking for me, I'll be in my studio trying something new.

Best,

Vivika

CHAPTER **1**

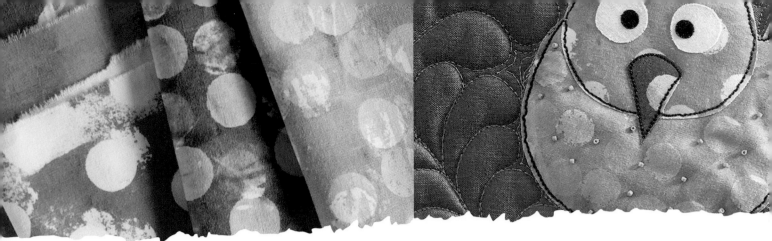

MAKE IT *colorful*

DYEING, PAINTING, PRINTING AND MORE

LAYERED MARBLING

A multicolored exploration in surface design.

jo fitsell

Marbling is an ancient technique of floating very thin paint on the surface of thickened water. The paint is then absorbed by placing fabric on the surface of the water, creating a design. Inspired by the way painters painstakingly layer each color on an oil painting, I experimented with increasing the layers of acrylic paint on my marbled fabrics to achieve a richer depth of color. By letting the fabric dry completely after each layer of paint was applied to the fabric, and floating stencils on the surface to capture colors, I was able to achieve great results. This process requires some preparation and patience, but the actual application is quick and addictive.

TOP TO BOTTOM:

Color for Lili (detail)

Revisiting the Meadow (detail)
Layered marbling, acrylic on canvas and cotton, acrylic resist; machine quilted.

MATERIALS

- Cotton fabric, cut to the size of your pan
- Fluid acrylic paint (such as Golden Artist Colors)
- Carageenan
- Alum
- Water
- Newspaper or newsprint
- Mild dish soap
- Gallon (3.8 L) container
- Blender
- Face mask
- Gloves
- Plastic tray (2" [5 cm] deep, transparent or white)
- Eyedroppers or squeeze bottles
- Fan
- Drying rack

▽ **SAFETY NOTE:** Wear gloves and a face mask if you have a sensitivity to alum.

Alum Soak

Before marbling, you need to soak your fabric in a solution containing water and alum. (Alum helps the paint adhere to the fabric. Soak your fabric before you cut it.)

1. Fill a sink with 2 gallons (7.6 L) of lukewarm water and add 2 tablespoons (30 mL) of alum.

2. Stir the alum into the water, then add your fabric and allow it to soak for 10–15 minutes. You can soak up to 4 yards (3.7 m) of fabric in this solution.

3. Without rinsing, remove your fabric and hang it on a clothesline to dry.

| NOTE: *You can soak fabric in the washing machine as long as you stop the rinse cycle. (It is important not to rinse the alum out.)*

4. When the fabric is dry and wrinkle-free, cut it to the size of your pan. You can also iron the fabric at this stage to remove wrinkles.

Prepare the Carageenan

Carageenan is made from seaweed and serves as a thickening agent. When handling carageenan, follow the warning labels on the package and wear a face mask to avoid breathing it in.

| NOTE: *The basic proportions are 2 tablespoons (30 mL) of carageenan to 1 gallon (3.8 L) of lukewarm water.*

1. Fill a gallon (3.8 L) container with lukewarm water and then use it to fill your blender halfway.

2. Add 1 tablespoon (15 mL) of carageenan to the blender and blend for approximately 1 minute, until the specks disappear.

3. Pour the carageenan mixture into your tray. Repeat this process with another tablespoon (15 mL) of carageenan, again filling the blender halfway. Pour the remaining water from your gallon (3.8 L) container into your tray.

4. Gently stir the mixture and let it sit until the bubbles are gone. The mixture should turn to a clear consistency. If bubbles persist, drag a strip of newspaper across the surface of the water to remove them..

| NOTE: *If you do not have a blender, just prepare the mixture the night before and let it sit. (I prepare 2 gallons [7.6 L] for my 16" × 20" [40.5 cm × 51 cm] tray. One gallon [3.8 L] is enough for a dish tray.)*

"

Marbling is an ancient technique of floating very thin paint on the surface of thickened water.

"

Marbling Technique

1. It is important to test your paint to see if it floats on the surface of the mixture. To prepare a test sample of paint, add a small amount of water to the paint using a ratio of 1 part water to 3 parts paint. Test the paint by dropping small amounts of it in the tray with an eyedropper or squeeze bottle (**FIGURE 1**). If your paint sinks to the bottom (**FIGURE 2**), continue diluting it with water until it spreads across the surface. Each paint will behave differently, so it is essential to take the time to test your paint until you find the correct water-to-paint ratio.

2. Using an eyedropper or squeeze bottle, drop your paint one drop at a time into the mixture. You will notice that the floating paint will begin to spread less as the surface is loaded and that it is possible to add colors on top of each other. Keep in mind that the first color you drop will spread the most (**FIGURE 3**).

3. When you have arranged paint on the surface in a design you like, hold your fabric in a "U" shape over the top of the pan (**FIGURE 4**). Lower the fabric from the center outwards, letting the fabric rest on the surface of the mixture. The paint will attach instantaneously. Lift your fabric up off the surface and place it on a sheet of newsprint.

4. Let your fabric dry for 24 hours. (A drying rack and fan work well.)

| **TIP:** *As you repeat the marbling, spend a little time beforehand looking at the piece and planning what colors to place on the next layer.*

5. When the fabric is dry, gently rinse it to remove the alum and carageenan. Do this in a sink filled with lukewarm water and a small amount of mild dish soap. Do not agitate the water or put the fabric under a running tap. Lay flat to dry. Press on the reverse side.

6. Repeat the marbling process for more layering effects. You do not need to add more alum to your fabrics on the second go around.

| OPTION: *Prepare and float stencils (made from lightweight cardboard or paper) on the surface, and add small amounts of paint inside each area (**FIGURE 5**). Lay fabric down on top of the stencil. Gently pat the back of the fabric to make sure the paint is attaching. You will see the fabric change color as it becomes wet (**FIGURE 6**).*

Finishing

You can reuse your carageenan mixture, though it will start to cloud. Carageenan may be saved for a few days in a cool space or placed in the refrigerator for months. To collect paint that has dropped to the bottom, pour off the carageenan mixture (I dispose of it in the toilet), and then place fabric on the bottom of the pan, as if you were monoprinting. The fabric will absorb the paint and you will have a fun, printed piece.

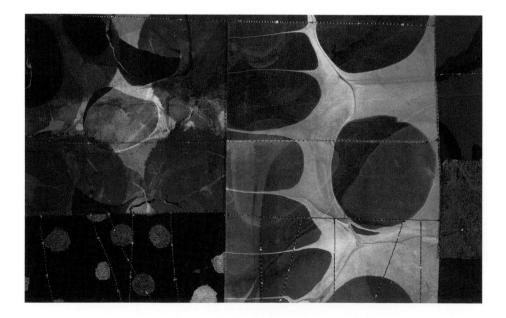

FIG. 1

FIG. 2

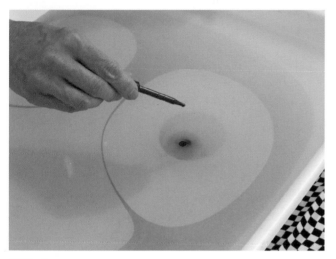

FIG. 3

FIG. 4

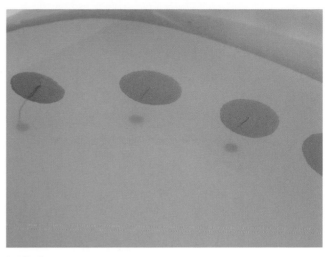

FIG. 5

FIG. 6

MOLDABLE FOAM STAMPS & STENCILS

Make your own surface design tools for printing fabric.

traci bunkers

I love to make my own stamps and stencils out of inexpensive, repurposed items. Stamps and stencils are a fun and easy way to print your own fabric. They can be used to create backgrounds and graphics for art cloth, or to liven up your quilting stash.

I often use printed fabrics—whether I'm working in my art journal, creating a mixed-media painting, or making art cloth—because I like to layer my work and printed fabrics give me a head start. (Be sure to wash your fabric before printing to remove any sizing. After drying, iron to remove wrinkles for a smooth printing surface.)

Before stamping or stenciling onto fabric it is also a good idea to cover your work surface with plastic or wax paper. This will protect your table from any paint or ink that might soak through the fabric. When you are finished printing or stenciling your fabric, follow the manufacturer's directions for the fabric paint or stamp pads before washing the fabric.

Hopefully, this gives you some ideas on easy ways to print your own fabrics. Have fun experimenting, and keep your eyes open for new items to repurpose into printing tools or stencils.

- Cotton fabric (washed and ironed)

FOR MOLDABLE-FOAM STAMPS

- Foam flip-flops
- Fabric paint (I used Jacquard Textile Color, Lumiere, and Tulip soft fabric paint)
- Permanent stamp pads for fabric (I use VersaCraft, Staz-On, and ColorBox)
- Plastic drop cloth or wax paper
- Scissors
- Craft knife
- Cutting mat
- Steel ruler
- Heat-embossing tool
- Textured items for molding the stamps
- Brayer hand tool
- Paint palette
- Baby wipes

FOR STENCILING

- Fabric paint
- Fabric spray paint (I use Tulip fabric spray paint.)
- Items to use as stencils
- Paint palette, wax paper, or foam plate
- Paintbrush or stencil brush (Cheap, round brushes work fine.)

SAFETY NOTES:
- Don't hold the foam while heating it or you'll burn your fingers.
- When working with spray paint make sure to work in a well-ventilated area.

Moldable-Foam Stamps

Moldable foam is a type of foam that, when heated, takes on the texture of whatever it is pressed against, keeping an impression until it is reheated. You can use all kinds of foam objects to create moldable-foam stamps. The most surprising, cheapest, and easiest foam objects to use are flip-flops. One pair of flip-flops will yield many stamps.

Prepare the Flip-Flop

Before using the flip-flop as a stamp, it will need to be cut into smaller pieces. Big pieces of foam are hard to evenly heat and keep hot before molding. For best results, use pieces no larger than 4" (10 cm) square.

1. Using a pair of scissors and with the top surface of the flip-flop facing up, cut off the straps as close to the surface of the flip-flop as possible and push out the part that goes through the foam to the bottom.

2. Working with the flip-flop on top of a cutting mat, place a steel ruler where you want to cut. Hold the ruler down with one hand, and with the other hand, cut against it with a craft knife. Try to hold the knife perpendicular to the flip-flop so you aren't cutting at an angle.

Make the Stamp

You will have to work quickly once the foam is heated. An easy way to arrange the items (to save time) is to trace around the stamp on a piece of paper. Arrange your items on the paper using the outline as a template. You can use just about anything for the textured item to mold the foam.

1. Lay the foam down with the smooth (top) surface facing up.

2. Use a heat-embossing tool to heat the surface of the foam for 5–10 seconds. (The smaller the piece of foam, the less time it will take to heat.)

3. Quickly place the heated surface on top of your textured item(s), press down (applying pressure), and hold for 5 seconds.

4. Check the impression. If necessary, reheat the foam and try again.

| **TIP:** *Sometimes it's easier to apply even pressure on the foam by pressing down on it with a piece of wood or a book.*

These pieces of foam are ready to mold.

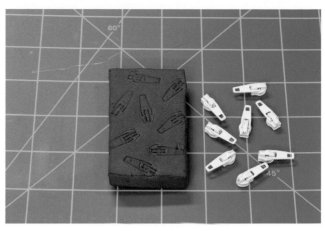

The stamp is molded by pressing the foam onto textured items.

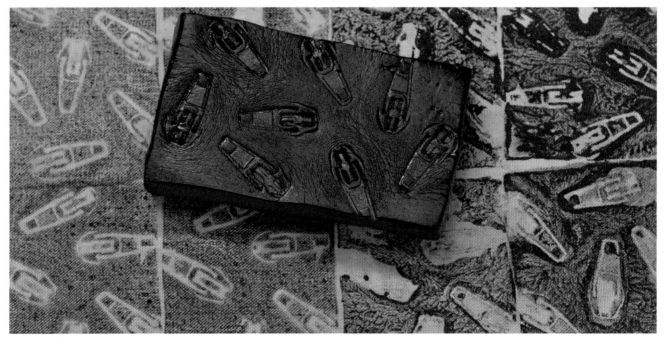

Process photos by Trcci Bunkers

The molded-foam stamp creates wonderful print designs on fabric. The left side was printed using a stamp pad.
The right side was printed with fabric paint.

Print with the Stamp

Your molded-foam stamp can be printed with paint or stamp pads. Paints will yield a grungier print while stamp pads will give a softer, more detailed print. To print with paint, apply it to the surface of the stamp with a brayer as follows.

1. Put a small amount of paint onto a paint palette. (Plexiglas, wax paper, or a plastic place mat may be used.)

2. Roll a brayer over the paint to evenly apply the paint to the roller.

3. Roll the charged brayer over the stamp, either while holding the stamp in your hand or while holding it on the paint palette.

4. Press the stamp onto the fabric, pressing down with your fingers over the whole stamp to be sure the entire surface prints. Reapply paint before stamping again.

| **TIP:** *When using paint, moldable-foam stamps may get clogged during the printing session and need to be cleaned. Removing the paint with a baby wipe will do the trick.*

A bubble wand can be used as a stencil.

Die-cut scrapbook paper can be used as a stencil.

Rug canvas can be used as a stencil.

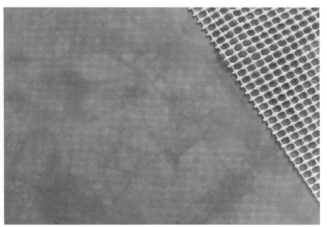

A soft pattern can be achieved by using fabric spray paint.

Stenciling

Almost anything can be used as a stencil as long as it will hold up to paint, is not too thick, and has holes or areas cut out. A few items I've used include die-cut scrapbook paper, die-cut craft felt, and a bubble wand. You can stencil using paint and a paintbrush, or spray paint.

When stenciling an allover repeating pattern, stencil the whole area except the edges. Then move the stencil over as far as possible, match up the design, and continue stenciling. If the paint is too wet, let it dry before proceeding.

Stenciling with a Paintbrush and Paint

1. Put some paint onto a paint palette, wax paper, or a foam plate.

2. Dab the brush into the paint on the palette, then tap the tip onto the palette to remove any extra paint. (It's best to not have too much paint on the brush.)

3. Lay the stencil on the fabric where you want it.

4. Holding the edges of the stencil with one hand and the brush straight up with the other hand, tap the brush on top of the stencil to push the paint through the open areas.

5. Move the brush around, adding more paint if needed, until the desired area is stenciled.

6. Move the stencil to the next area and repeat.

Stenciling with Fabric Spray Paint

1. Place the stencil on the fabric where you want your design.

2. Hold the stencil edges flat with one hand while spraying the desired area with the other.

3. Move the stencil to the next area and repeat.

“
Stamps can be used to create
backgrounds and graphics
for art cloth, or to liven up your
quilting stash.

”

COLORING CLOTH

Create surface design with food coloring and glue gel resist.

margarita korioth

In my small town, there are no art supply stores nearby. Since my artwork frequently starts with white fabric—because it gives me the freedom to create any design I want in any color I want—I have had to carefully plan my surface design projects, sometimes making do with what is around the house. This limitation inspired creativity, though, and led me to devise this coloring technique using items from my pantry and medicine cabinet.

My method is a twist on using school glue gel as a resist. When I first tried using a stencil to apply the glue to fabric, I couldn't see where the glue had been applied once it was dried. Mixing a few drops of liquid food coloring into the glue did the trick. I could see the resist on the fabric and yet the food coloring washed away with the glue gel—leaving no stain. My food-colored glue gel technique allows precise control, and can make shapes that are very distinct.

MATERIALS

- PFD (prepared for dyeing) cotton fabric, fat quarter (18" × 21" [45.5 cm × 53.5 cm])

- Liquid fabric paint (I used Dye-na-Flow from Jacquard.)

- Blue school glue gel

- Liquid food coloring

- Newspapers

- Batting, 20" × 30" (51 cm × 76 cm)

- Drop cloth or muslin, 1¼ yards (1 m)

- Painter's tape

- Prepared for dyeing (PFD) cotton fabric, fat quarter

- Small plastic containers and plastic spoons

- Eye dropper or pipette

- Small silk screen frame (I used a 10" × 12" [25.5 cm × 30.5 cm] frame.)

- Stencil (Use a stencil close in size to the silk screen frame.)

- Old credit card or squeegee

- Clear aloe vera gel or matte medium

OPTIONAL

- Foam brush

Prepare the Printing Surface

1. Stack the newspapers on top of each other and top with the batting. Place the drop cloth or muslin on this stack, wrap the edges around to the back of the newspaper/batting stack, and tape it in place with the painter's tape.

| NOTE: *My surface is 20" × 30" (51 cm × 76 cm) but customize yours to fit your space.*

2. Tape the printing surface to the worktable with painter's tape to keep it from shifting while printing.

Apply the Resist

3. Iron the PFD fabric. Pin or tape it to the printing surface.

4. Pour ⅓ cup (80 mL) of blue school glue gel into a small container. Use the eye dropper or pipette to add 2–3 drops of liquid food coloring. Mix well with a plastic spoon (**FIGURE 1**).

5. Tape the stencil to the underside of the silkscreen frame with painter's tape (**FIGURE 2**).

| **TIP:** *Use a stencil with a fairly simple design and large openings. Fine details may not transfer well.*

6. Pour some of the colored school glue gel into the well of the frame. Using an old credit card or a squeegee, drag the glue gel across the silk surface. This will push the resist through the stencil onto the fabric (**FIGURE 3**).

7. If you are finished applying resist to fabric, remove the silk screen and clean it and the stencil immediately. Set the fabric aside to air dry. This may take 24 hours.

8. When the fabric is thoroughly dry, heat set the glue by pressing with a dry iron (no steam) at medium heat from both sides. Do not skip this step—even though the glue is dry it needs to be heat set to obtain a clear resist.

TIPS FOR SUCCESS

- Use only liquid food coloring for this technique. The gel kind is almost impossible to remove from the fabric.

- If you want to use this technique on silk fabric, choose green, red, or yellow food coloring to mix with the glue gel. Blue food coloring tints the fabric and will not wash out.

FIG. 1

FIG. 2

FIG. 3

FIG. 4

FIG. 5

Paint the Fabric

9. In another small container, mix 1 tablespoon (14.8 mL) clear aloe vera gel and ½ teaspoon (2.5 mL) of liquid fabric paint. Mix well with a plastic spoon (**FIGURE 4**).

| **TIP:** *I like to use Dye-na-Flow because it is a highly pigmented liquid paint. You only need a small amount of paint to color cloth, which makes it ideal for this technique.*

10. Pin the fabric with the glue gel facing up on the printing surface. Use the credit card, squeegee, or foam brush to move the paint across the cloth (**FIGURE 5**). Set it aside to dry. This usually takes 6–12 hours.

11. Once dry, heat set the fabric from both sides with a dry iron, following the manufacturer's instructions.

12. Soak the fabric in water for an hour and then wash it by hand or in a washing machine with a mild detergent. Air dry and press. Your fabric is ready for your next project!

PATTERN PLAY

Fabric design with itajime dyeing.

jeanne aird

I started working with tie-dyeing in the 1970s and began researching shibori techniques a few years ago. I was greatly inspired by the book *Shibori: The Inventive Art of Japanese Shaped Resist Dyeing* by Yoshiko Iwamoto Wada, Mary Kellogg Rice, and Jane Barton and have been experimenting ever since.

Itajime is just one of many shibori techniques. Shibori is an ancient Japanese method of creating pattern on fabric through manipulating it to resist dye. In itajime, clamps are used to secure folded fabric, often with shapes clamped above and below the fabric bundle that act as resists to the dye.

Just like unwrapping a present, there is always a surprise when you unclamp the dyed fabric and see the results. To a certain extent you can plan how you want the fabric to turn out but, due to the nature of the dyeing process, there is always serendipity in the final fabric. Subtle nuances of color where dyes have migrated and new patterns created by unexpected folds or mixtures of color keep the fabrics you create fresh and unique.

Rather than immersing the fabric in a dye bath as many artists do, I prefer the more intense colors and intentional patterns that I achieve by applying dye directly onto the clamped fabric.

MATERIALS

| NOTE: *All supplies must be dedicated to nonfood use.*

- Cotton or silk PFD (prepared for dyeing) fabric (I like to work with ½ yard [0.5 m] cuts.)

- Synthrapol (by Jacquard)

- Urea

- Soda ash

- Procion MX dyes (Jacquard Products), 2 ounces (56 g) each of 4 colors

- Dust mask or respirator

- Rubber gloves

- Large bowl for rinsing tools

- Plastic drop cloth or sheeting

- Measuring spoons and cups

- Plastic containers with tight-fitting lids, 1 quart-size (1 L) container and 4 pint-size (473 mL) containers

- Plastic spoons

- Plastic funnel

- 4 plastic squeeze bottles, 8 ounce (237 mL) size

- Long-handled spoon

- 5-gallon (19 L) bucket

- Clamps

- Pairs of shapes for clamping such as ceramic tiles, jar lids, washers, wood blocks and strips, CDs, etc.

- Rags

▽ CAUTION: Always wear a dust mask or respirator and rubber gloves when working with chemicals and powdered dyes.

Prepare the Work Space

1. Cover your work area with a plastic drop cloth or a sheet of painter's plastic.

2. Fill a large bowl with water and set it in a convenient location for rinsing your gloved hands and tools.

| NOTE: *Rinse your gloved hands frequently so you don't contaminate the colors. Put your tools in the bowl immediately after using them and wipe down your work surface often with a damp rag to keep it clean and prevent fabrics from picking up unwanted dyes.*

Prepare the Dye

1. Mix 8 tablespoons (118.5 mL) of urea with 1 quart (1 L) of warm (not hot) water in a plastic container with a tight-fitting lid. Shake the mixture to dissolve the urea. Let it cool to room temperature before using.

2. Mix the liquid dye concentrate by measuring 2 tablespoons (30 mL) of dye powder into a plastic pint (473 mL) container. (Some dyes, like turquoise and black, require more dye, so refer to the directions from the manufacturer.) Gradually add 1 cup (237 mL) of the mixed urea solution to the dye powder a little at a time, stirring with a plastic spoon to make a paste so the dye dissolves thoroughly. Mix 4 different colors total.

3. Using a funnel, pour ¼ cup (60 mL) of the urea solution and ¼ cup (60 mL) of liquid dye concentrate into a squeeze bottle. Cap the bottle tightly and mix the solution by shaking. Mix the remaining 3 colors of dye. This should be enough to dye ½ yard (0.5 m) of fabric.

4. To prepare the soda ash solution, mix 1½ cups (209 g) plus 3 tablespoons (26 g) of soda ash with 3 gallons (11.4 L) of warm water in the 5-gallon (19 L) bucket. Stir the solution with a long-handled spoon until the soda ash is dissolved.

| TIP: *To make a different amount of solution, the recipe is 9 tablespoons (78.5 g) of soda ash per gallon (3.8 L) of warm water.*

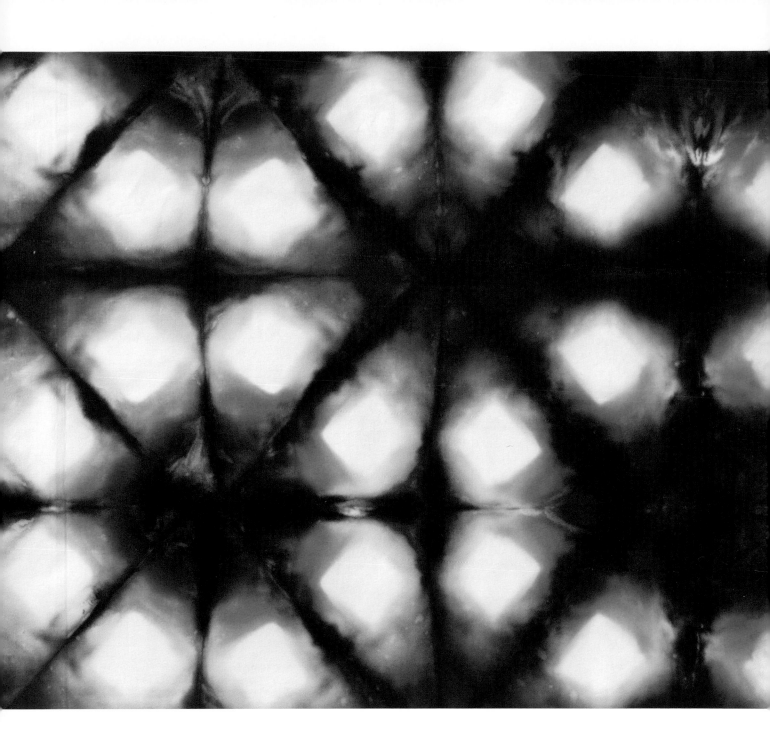

"

Shibori is an ancient Japanese
method of creating pattern
on fabric through manipulating
it to resist dye.

"

Fold, Clamp, and Soak the Fabric

1. Using ½-yard (0.5 m) lengths of fabric and starting with the longer side, accordion fold the fabric twice, creating 3 layers.

2. Starting at a short end, fold the corner up to the opposite side to create a triangular edge (**FIGURE 1**).

3. Continue to accordion fold the fabric in a triangular fashion, similar to folding a flag. Using an iron helps keep the folds more regular for the whole length (**FIGURE 2**).

4. Position the shapes you want to use as resists on the top and bottom of the folded fabric. Make sure they line up precisely with each other. Use a clamp to hold them tightly in place. In this sample, a 2" (5 cm) square ceramic tile was clamped to either side of the folded fabric (**FIGURE 3**).

5. Submerge the clamped fabric in the soda ash solution and allow the fabric to soak for 15–30 minutes.

Materials for creating Pattern Play designs.

Dye and Cure the Fabric

1. Cover your work surface with a clean sheet of plastic that is about 2–3 times larger than the clamped fabric.

2. Remove the clamped fabric from the soda ash solution, gently squeezing out excess water.

3. Place the clamped fabric in the center of the plastic. Using the diluted dye in squeeze bottles, squeeze the color where desired. For the sample, I applied yellow close to the tiles, then orange, then red, followed by black squeezed on the outside edges of the triangle (**FIGURE 4**).

4. Gently turn the clamped piece over and apply more dye in a similar sequence to the opposite side. Squeeze more dye into the folds by gently lifting and separating them.

5. As excess dye accumulates on the plastic, mop it up with a rag so the colors don't get muddy.

6. Wrap the clamped fabric in the plastic you used to cover your work surface. Place it in a plastic container and let it cure for 24 hours. The fabric should be kept at approximately 70° F (21° C). Don't let it get too cold or too hot.

Rinse the Fabric

1. After the fabric has cured, remove the clamps and shapes and put them in the rinse bowl. Rinse the fabric in cool water to remove the soda ash solution and excess dye. Repeat the rinsing process with warm water and, finally, with hot water.

2. Wash the fabric twice by machine using hot water and Synthrapol. To test if all the dye has been removed, sandwich the dyed fabric between two pieces of white fabric and iron the layers together. If color transfers to the white fabric, wash the dyed fabric again.

3. Consider this project as a starting point. There are countless different shapes and folding patterns to experiment with.

FIG. 1

FIG. 2

FIG. 3

FIG. 4

JEANNE'S TIPS TO DYE FOR

- I like using mercerized fabric because it takes the dyes better. Colors appear brighter and deeper.

- Dyes will keep for a month or longer if refrigerated. I keep mine in a little dorm-size fridge—away from food—in our barn. Just be sure to label each container with its specific contents: dye concentrate or diluted dye. Bring the dye to room temperature before using it again.

- Mixed urea will last for months at room temperature. Discard it when it smells like ammonia.

- I keep a covered bucket of prepared soda ash solution outside and reuse it for months.

- This folding and clamping technique can also be used to discharge dyes from fabric and to over-dye colored fabric as well.

OUTDOOR FLAT DYEING

Techniques for fabulous results.

robin ferrier

Nothing says it's summer more than being outdoors. Even where I live—in Hawaii, where the sun shines most of the year—I get a special feeling about those long halcyon days. There is nothing more peaceful and satisfying than moving my dye studio outside so I can enjoy the sunshine and create hand-dyed fabric. I was first lured outside by necessity several years ago. Having a young family and being concerned about using potentially harmful chemicals in the house, venturing outside seemed like a practical solution. When dyeing outdoors, I can lay out fabric, arrange dye solution, and clean my supplies with less worry about creating a mess or exposure to airborne dye. Best of all, most of the energy required to create these unique fabrics is supplied by the sun.

The type of dyeing that I prefer, flat dyeing, is actually a method of low-immersion dyeing done on a flat surface. This is not a new concept, but it's one I've refined to suit not only the type of work I do, but also the space and materials I have to work with. The results of this dye technique are gorgeous hand-dyed solid fabrics with a slightly mottled texture.

Photos by Robin Ferrier

Elements #25 (detail)

MATERIALS

| NOTE: *All supplies must be dedicated to nonfood use.*

- PFD (prepared for dyeing) fabric, (6) 1 yard (0.9 m) lengths (see tip below)

- Procion MX dyes (Jacquard Products), 2 oz. (56 g) each in the colors of your choice

- Soda ash

- Synthrapol (by Jacquard)

- Rock salt (optional)

- Dust mask and rubber gloves

- Measuring cup and measuring spoons

- Plastic dishpan

- Container to hold clear water for rinsing gloves

- Mason jars with lids, 1 per dye color

- Heavy-weight painter's plastic, cut into 8 approximately 4' (1.2 m) square pieces

- Paint roller

| **TIP:** *I use Pimatex cotton PFD fabric because it has a tight weave that absorbs dye well and irons smoothly when finished. PFD stands for "prepared for dyeing" and refers to fabric that has no optical whiteners or other finishes that may interfere with the dyeing process. Since I dye so much fabric, I order it by the bolt.*

SAFETY NOTES: Dye powder requires caution since it is very fine and can become airborne. Always wear a dust mask or respirator and rubber gloves when working with chemicals and powdered dyes. Working in an open area with no wind is very important.

Prepare the Dye

1. Mix 1 cup (237 mL) of soda ash with 1 gallon (3.8 L) of water in a large bucket. Soak the fabric in the soda ash solution until it is fully saturated.

2. Set your washing machine to spin and drain, making sure to shut off the water valve to the washer so the washing machine doesn't rinse as it spins. Spin out all the excess soda ash solution, and set the fabric aside.

3. Mix your dyes by adding 6 teaspoons (30 mL) of dye to 1½ cups (355 ml) of water in each mason jar. Each jar contains enough to dye 1 yard (0.9 m) of fabric. At this stage I throw 2 tablespoons (36 g) of salt into each jar, being sure to mix until dissolved. (Continued on next spread)

WHY SOLID FABRIC?

The fabrics I dye are mostly solid in texture, but they are not too solid to be mistaken for a commercial fabric. There are some gentle variations in color, and sometimes there is a line where the fabric was folded during the dye process. As an artist, I appreciate fabric that speaks of the hand that dyed it. I make quilts with hand-dyed solid fabrics because I want the viewer to see my compositions without the distraction of patterned fabric. The mood in my quilts is conveyed through color, shape, balance, tension, and harmony. Having a hand in creating my own fabric is important to me as it allows me to make color choices with intention and keep my work timeless.

MATERIALS

- 1–2 large folding tables
- Heavyweight painter's plastic
- Large plastic buckets
- Water source

OPTIONAL

- Clothesline
- Rocks or bricks for weights

Creating a Temporary Outdoor Dye Studio

An outdoor studio can be set up relatively quickly when the spirit moves you to work in a natural setting. It doesn't take up much space, and it requires little in the way of special equipment. All of the supplies you need are identical to those you would use in an indoor wet studio, but there are a few major advantages to working in the open air. Namely, cleanup is much easier and the sunlight provides all of the energy required.

1. Position the dyeing table in an area that gets full sunlight. For practical purposes, I prefer to set it on a little bit of a downhill slant so that when excess dye is squeezed out of the fabric, it will drain away from where I am working.

2. Place an old cutting mat on top of the table, then cover it with a sheet of heavy painter's plastic.

| NOTE: *If you do not have a running water source available such as a faucet or hose, be sure to have several buckets of water at the ready for rinsing gloves and supplies.*

3. Position an extra table or shelf nearby to hold your supplies.

4. You now have a temporary dye studio ready to go! Gather your materials and prepare to master the basics of flat dyeing in your temporary work space. The accompanying instructions will lead you through dyeing 6 yards (5.5 m) of fabric, but you can easily increase the amount of fabric and dye.

Dye and Cure Fabric

4. Lay out a piece of fabric on your dyeing surface and fold in half.

5. Pour the first dye solution onto the fabric and spread around with gloved hands until the dye water saturates the fabric evenly (**FIGURE 1**). Rinse your gloved hands to remove any traces of dye.

6. Place a 4′ (1.2 m) square piece of plastic on top of the dyed fabric, covering it entirely. Smooth out the bubbles with the paint roller, allowing any excess dye to run off the end of the table (**FIGURE 2**).

| NOTE: *Using this method of flat dyeing, all of these fabrics can be dyed at the same time because they are separated by a plastic barrier.*

7. Repeat steps 4–6 until all of your fabric is stacked and covered in dye. (You can dye up to 20 yards [18.3 m] of fabric in one dye session using this process, but I usually work with about a dozen.)

8. Allow the stack to "bake" in the sunlight for a day. Pile rocks or something heavy on top of the stack in case of windy weather.

9. The next day, take apart your layers, throwing the fabric into a water-filled bucket and tossing the plastic into a pile to be rinsed later.

10. Rinse the fabric outside in a bucket or with a hose. Squeeze out the excess fluid and then wash in the washing machine with synthrapol. The fabric can be dried on a clothesline or in the dryer.

FIG. 1

FIG. 2

" Best of all, most of the energy
required to create these unique
fabrics is supplied by the sun. "

CHAPTER **2**

MIX IT *up!*

MIXED-MEDIA QUILTING
TECHNIQUES

FIRST MAKE A CUP OF TEA

Turn upcycled tea bags into a creative canvas.

libby williamson

Steamy tea and a good book on a rainy day provide more than blissful comfort. The overlooked bonus is the lowly tea bag, often discarded without a thought. This substrate, stained in lovely hues of ochre and sepia, begs to be adorned with fabric, thread, and paint.

Tea bags were an accidental invention attributed by some to an early American tea merchant who gave sample-sized silk pouches of tea to his customers. His intention, though, was misunderstood. Rather than emptying the contents into strainers, some dropped entire bags into the pot. Thus the convenient, disposable tea bag was born. Lucky us. More art supplies!

Today's tea bags are made from various fibers, most commonly abaca, the leaf stalk of the banana plant. The resulting paper is surprisingly strong, able to withstand boiling water, and sometimes a wringing squeeze.

The shape and construction of teabags varies. Some have folded tops with tiny staples used to fasten a tag with string. There are stringless pillow-shaped bags with the tea sealed inside. Some bags are round, others have multiple compartments for the tea leaves. I have played with them all.

For this project I chose square, stringless bags. The shape provided a straight edge for binding. These tea bags have a ¼" (6 mm) glued perimeter with an embossed linear pattern, creating a frame around the edge of each art piece. The bags I used contained peppermint tea. Some fruity herbal teas will stain in interesting bright pink shades; black tea yields a darker tone.

MATERIALS

- Used tea bags
- Unbleached muslin scraps
- Liquid matte medium
- Black sewing thread
- Sewing machine with free-motion capability
- White gesso
- Acrylic paint
- Small paintbrush
- Toothpick or skewer
- Cotton swab

OPTIONAL

- Tiny scraps of fabric and thin paper for collage
- Crochet thread and large-eye needle for assembly

Create Your Canvas

1. Brew your tea and enjoy! I save up my bags so that I can work on several pieces simultaneously.

2. Completely dry the bags with the tea leaves inside. Using small, sharp scissors, carefully cut a small slit through the top layer of paper along one vertical edge. Try not to cut through both layers. Make the slit as close as possible to the sealed side. Expand the slit along the edge, stopping at the sealed glue line (**FIGURE 1**).

3. Empty out the tea. (I add mine to my plants as fertilizer.) A small paintbrush will help release any stubborn leaves.

4. Cut a piece of muslin slightly smaller than the inside of the pocket to use as a liner. Unravel the muslin edges a little so they blend in. Insert the liner by folding it over your finger and sliding it gently between the layers of the tea bag. Using a skewer or toothpick and a damp cotton swab, maneuver the fabric into place, aligning it with the edges and easing it into the corners (**FIGURE 2**).

5. With a small paintbrush, spread a drop of matte medium along the open seam to seal the bag closed (**FIGURE 3**). Let dry. Flip the tea bag over so the mended side is on the back.

| NOTE: *If you are planning to finish the tea bags as a book, position the glued edges on the left side so they will be hidden in the bookbinding.*

6. Collage thin papers or bits of fabric onto the surface of the tea bag with matte medium. Let dry before stitching (**FIGURE 4**).

7. Using black thread for the top feed and bobbin, machine stitch the design. Stitch within the stabilized area to avoid paper tears. Trim threads.

| TIP: *Start with simple designs before attempting more intricate images. Add more detail with paint, or sketch the design using a water-soluble fabric marker.*

8. Depending on the degree of tea stains on the paper, apply gesso to restore the "white" of the paper. The paint will show up as brighter colors. Alternately, natural (non-gessoed) bags will yield lovely muted paintings. Apply gesso and acrylic paints with tiny brushes in thin layers inside the stitched lines. Let each layer of paint dry before applying the next.

FIG. 1

FIG. 2

FIG. 3

FIG. 4

FIG. 5

Finishing

Enjoy your adorned tea bags as individual tiny treasures—
or try these finishing techniques.

Book Assembly

1. Align the edges of 5 bags and pin together **(FIGURE 5)**.

2. Using free-motion or straight stitch, sew through all layers along the left edge to bind the book.

Bunting Assembly

1. Thread a handsewing needle with crochet thread and carefully pierce the top corner of the tea bag.

| **TIP:** *Catch the muslin in this stitch. If you pierce too close to the edge, the paper may tear.*

2. Cut the thread to about 8" (20.5 cm) long and tie a simple overhand knot about ¼" (6 mm) above the paper edge. Trim the thread tails. Gently rotate the knot to the back of the tea bag **(FIGURE 6)**. Make a thread loop at the other top corner.

3. Make thread loops on each tea bag for the bunting.

4. Cut a 24" (61 cm) piece of crochet thread and thread it through all of the loops, stringing the bags together. Add a tiny drop of matte medium at the top of each thread loop if the bags slide together.

FIG. 6

SPIN-ART SURFACE DESIGN

Experiment with a carnival of color.

lynda heines

From the moment I first fell in love with surface design, I have been on the lookout for new ways to create original fabric for my stash. Several years ago I found an art spinner in the toy section of a local discount store. That toy brought back fond memories of childhood carnival days, when I visited the spin-art booth and added paint on top of spinning paper in a large metal drum. One of the most exciting things about spin art was that the final result was always a surprise. No two pieces were ever exactly alike.

I had high hopes that with my new spin-art machine, I could reproduce some of those little artworks that I had loved making as a child. At first, I played with the technique using paper—its intended use—and produced some lovely pages for my journal. But I knew I needed to take this technique one step further and experiment on fabric.

MATERIALS

| NOTE: *This is a comprehensive list for all of the techniques covered here.*

- Fabric, prewashed, ironed, and cut into 6" [15 cm] squares

- Fabric paint or ink (Any paint or ink that you use on fabric can be used in this technique. I used thinned Jacquard Textile Color, Dye-Na-Flow, and Lumiere paints.)

- Spray fabric paint (I used Simply Spray.)

- Painter's tape

- White glue , such as Elmer's Washable School Glue

- Watercolor paper, cut into 5½" (14 cm) squares

- Spin-art machine (A battery-operated machine is required. Self-propelled versions and salad spinners don't give the same results. I used the Lite Brite Flash Art Neon Paint Spinner by Hasbro.)

- Covered workspace

- Several small watercolor brushes

- Spray bottle with water

- Squeeze bottles

- Paint palette

Basic Spin-Art Technique

| NOTE: *In order to make this technique work, you may need to alter the consistency of the paint. The paint should pour, but not be too thin.*

1. Attach a 6" (15 cm) square of fabric to the machine base with a loop of painter's tape. This is an important step. If the fabric is not attached, it will fly out of the machine or fold up on itself.

2. Turn on the machine. Using textile paints in squeeze bottles, drizzle paint onto the spinning fabric (**FIGURE 1**). This is an opportunity to play. You can squeeze the paint out in a circle or in lines.

3. Turn off the machine and check your progress. If you want to add more paint, turn the machine back on and continue to add additional colors.

4. When you are satisfied with the finished design, gently pull the fabric out of the spinner, and set it aside to dry.

5. After 24 hours, iron on the reverse side and it's ready to use.

Basic Spin-Art Designs

Concentric Circles

Concentric Circles

A fun technique that is easily achieved using the machine is making concentric circles.

1. Pour textile paints onto a paint palette.

2. Dip the tip of a small watercolor brush into the first paint color. Be sure to use a separate brush for each color.

3. Attach a square of fabric to the machine. While the machine is spinning, gently touch the brush tip to the fabric (**FIGURE 2**). Once you start adding paint, the circles will appear. Stop and start the machine and continue to add paint until you are happy with your design.

4. Remove the fabric from the machine and set it aside to cure for 24 hours.

5. Iron on wrong side to heat set.

| VARIATION: *After the circles are completed, turn the spinner back on. Drizzle paint over the spinning fabric, creating a layer of splatters over the circles.*

FIG. 1

FIG. 2

Watercolor Effects

Glue Resist

Watercolor Effects

This technique results in a design with the look of a watercolor painting.

1. Attach the fabric to the spinner and spray with water.

2. Turn on the machine. Squeeze thinned paint onto the spinning fabric. I used three colors, but you can use as many as you like. The water causes the paints to blend together for an entirely different look.

3. Remove the fabric from the spinner and set aside to dry for 24 hours.

4. Iron on wrong side to heat set.

Glue Resist

You can easily use a spin-art machine to create a resist that can later be painted for a one-of-a-kind surface design result.

1. Attach a square of fabric to the machine, turn it on, and then squeeze glue directly from the bottle over the spinning fabric. Continue spinning and adding glue until you are happy with the resist design. (Just like with the other techniques, you can stop the machine to check your design.)

2. Remove the fabric from the spinner and set it aside to dry for 24 hours.

3. Spray the glue-resist fabric with fabric spray paint. When you're happy with the coverage, allow the fabric to dry for 72 hours.

4. Rinse the fabric in lukewarm water. You may need to rub it with your fingers to remove the glue. After drying, the paint can be set by ironing.

Monoprinting

One of the negatives of spin art is that you are limited to the size of the fabric (no larger than 6" [15 cm] squares). However, you can create a monoprint on paper which can transfer the image to a larger piece of fabric.

1. Place a piece of fabric (any size) on a padded board next to the spinner.

2. Attach a 5½" (14 cm) square of watercolor paper to the spinner machine base with painter's masking tape.

3. Create a piece of spin art using fabric paints and any of the techniques. When you are satisfied with the design, remove the paper from the machine.

4. Place the finished paper face down on your fabric. Using a brayer, roll over the back of the paper to transfer the design onto the fabric. Remove the watercolor paper to reveal the image on your fabric.

5. Let the fabric dry for 24 hours, then heat set the image as you did for the other textile paint techniques.

| NOTE: *If you want to get a second "ghost" image from the paper, lightly spray the paper with water and place it face down on the fabric. The image will be much lighter.*

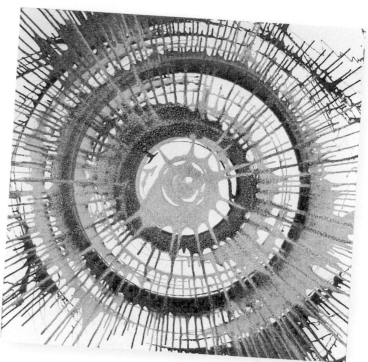

Monoprinting

MORE IDEAS FOR SPIN ART

REPURPOSE:
The watercolor paper used for monoprinting can be repurposed as a decorative page for your art journal.

LAYER:
Add a spin-art layer to previously dyed or stamped fabric.

CREATE:
Make spin-art rubbing plates by using dimensional paint on cardboard.

INTENSE ART CLOTH

Creating with layers of surface design and stitch.

lynn krawczyk

Having a treasure trove of surface-design techniques at your fingertips makes it possible to create endless variations of art cloth for your projects. For my art quilts, I create two different styles of art cloth, which I call low-intensity art cloth and high-intensity art cloth. Both styles are created by combining multiple surface-design techniques and incorporating stitch as an elemental layer.

This method is quite versatile, and you can add stitching at any stage of the process. However, if you wish to create art cloth similar to my samples, add the stitching according to these steps. Also, if you want to attach your fabric to canvas, choose the canvas size first and then cut your piece of fabric to fit before you begin working.

Examples of a low-intensity art cloth (left) and a high-intensity art cloth (right).

MATERIALS

- Cotton fabric
- Jacquard textile paint
- Fabric paint (I like Jacquard Dye-na-Flow paint)
- Sponge brush
- Paintbrush
- Plastic palette knife
- Thermofax screens (see Thermofax Prints sidebar for more information)
- Plaid Simply Screen paint
- Doily
- Found objects for stamping
- Short length of macramé cord
- Artist's canvas
- Iron and ironing board

OPTIONAL

- Lightweight fusible interfacing
- Sewing machine

Low-Intensity Art Cloth

Low-intensity art cloth works with colors that reside in the same color family. Color choices are simplified and guaranteed to work together because they live in the same area of the color wheel.

1. Choose 3 colors next to each other on the color wheel. For example, in the sample shown in **FIGURE 1**, I selected green, yellow (the base fabric color), and orange. You can add additional colors to your design by using shades and tones of these 3 colors.

2. To create the first layer, add stitching to your plain cotton fabric either by hand or machine. I don't use stabilizer when I stitch, because I don't mind the occasional ripple or pucker. If this bothers you, use a lightweight interfacing underneath the fabric as you stitch.

| **TIP:** *If you are using a machine and want to do very dense stitching, stop every so often and iron the fabric to help prevent ripples. If you are stitching by hand, thin sewing thread works best. Heavier embroidery thread will cause the paint to pool later when you print on top of it.*

3. The second layer breaks up the solid appearance of the fabric. To add this layer, dip a sponge brush in the fabric paint and make broad, random sweeps across the fabric. Use a color that is close to the color of your fabric (I used copper paint), and try to print off the edges of the fabric to avoid leaving an empty frame of space.

| NOTE: *After each layer of printing, allow the paint to dry completely before moving on to the next step. Also, ironing after each step will help keep your fabric flat and smooth as you add additional layers.*

OPACITY EXPLAINED

Opacity refers to whether or not you can see through the paint once it's applied to the fabric. High-opacity paint creates a solid print that blocks the fabric underneath. Low-opacity paint allows the fabric underneath (or any other print) to be seen through it. Using low-opacity paint creates a kind of sheer layer that adds interest, but doesn't stand out in a way that causes busyness. Experiment with using both types of paint.

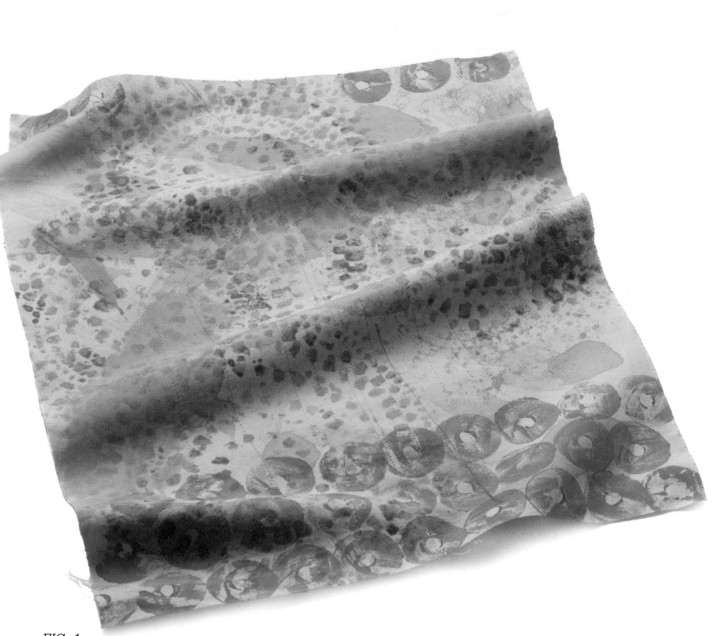

FIG. 1

4. The third layer incorporates monoprinting with a doily. Use one of the colors you chose that is next to the color of your base fabric. (I used olive green.) Doily monoprinting is a quick and easy way to add abstract pattern. To print, simply place the doily on top of your fabric and use a paintbrush to push paint through the openings. (Doilies with larger patterns work best.)

5. Using a found object, stamp a pattern to create the fourth layer. Select a paint color that is the highest contrast from the color group you chose. Stamp across some of the areas you printed in the second layer to

create a sense of depth. (For example, I used a mixture of orange and brown paint to get a deeper orange.)

6. Using a palette knife, create the fifth layer by making a wide, curved arc across the center portion of the fabric. Use the lowest contrast color you chose and paint that has low opacity. (I used Jacquard Ochre.) To apply the paint, use a plastic palette knife that has a step in it. Dip the knife into your fabric paint, gather a healthy amount of paint on the back side of the palette, and sweep the knife across the fabric in one motion.

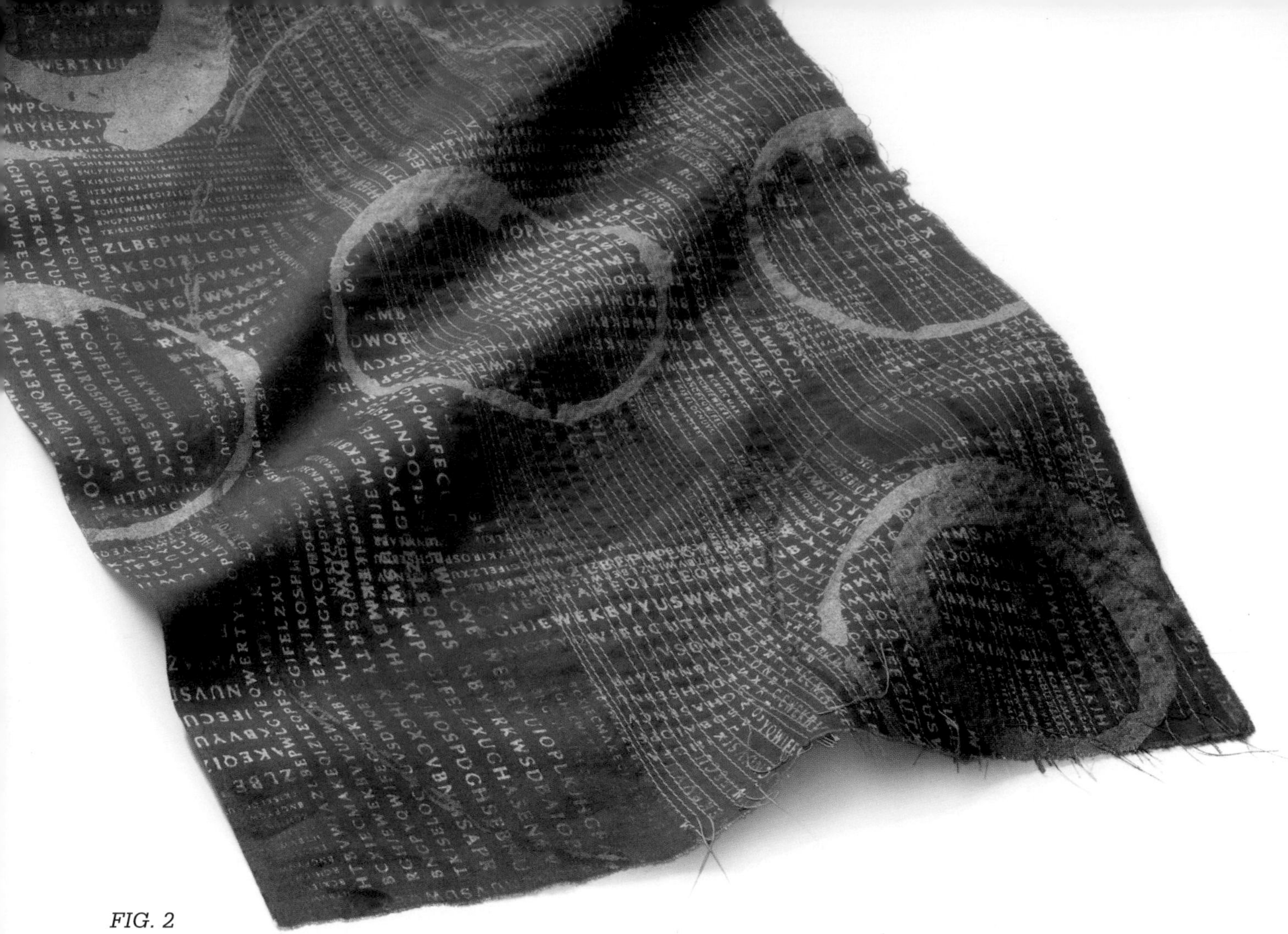

FIG. 2

High-Intensity Art Cloth

High-intensity art cloth is for graphic contrast junkies. The intent is to draw attention to every element put down on the cloth and create a piece of cloth that is full of energy. With the addition of stitching at different stages of layering, it is possible to add unexpected texture and visual interest.

1. Choose two colors that are on opposite sides of the color wheel. For example, for the sample shown in **FIGURE 2**, I chose purple and orange.
2. To create the first layer, create an uneven print of text using a Thermofax screen. (I used white paint.) See the Thermofax Prints sidebar for more information.

| **TIP:** *White will always cause a high degree of contrast when paired with medium to dark tones of any color on the color wheel.*

THERMOFAX PRINTS

Thermofax screen printing is a form of screen printing that uses Thermofax screens. These screens are created using a Thermofax machine and have an image permanently burned into them. To use a Thermofax screen:

1. Place the screen, shiny side down, against the fabric.
2. Squirt paint across the screen.
3. Brush the paint across the image with either a sponge brush or squeegee.

3. The second layer adds stitching either by hand or machine in a color that is in sharp contrast to the color of your fabric. (I used bright orange thread.)

4. To add the third layer, print on top of the stitching and the first layer in a color that is the same as one of the contrasting colors you chose in Step 1 (or close to it). In this case I did additional Thermofax screen printing in gold, which is a neighbor to the contrasting color of orange that was paired with the blue fabric.

5. Using a palette knife, swipe paint across your fabric in random areas to create the fourth layer. Use a paint color that is very close to your base fabric to help some of the contrast in the preceding layers fade in some areas. (I used blue paint.)

6. The fifth and final layer is used to add more contrast. Staying in the same color family, choose pale or bright versions of your color. Monoprint by dipping macramé cord into a pale shade of your selected color, and apply to your fabric to create monoprints in long, sweeping arcs. (You can easily line up the ends of the prints to make it appear like a long single print.)

| **TIP:** *A short length of cord is easier to control. I recommend a length of about 6" (15 cm).*

Display Your Art Cloth

Once you've created your masterpiece, it's time to decide how to display it. I like to attach my art cloth to canvas so it's ready to hang. To do the same:

1. Wrap a canvas in fabric. (This is another opportunity to add more color and interest. If you don't want to introduce a new color, use black or the same color as your base fabric, so that the canvas blends in.)

2. Attach your art cloth to the canvas by adding fusible web to the back of the fabric and then fusing it directly to the fabric on the canvas.

Surface design is a very liberating art form, allowing you to explore a wide variety of techniques and applications on fabric. Art cloth allows you to put all the different techniques you've learned together to create a truly unique piece of work that expresses your point of view.

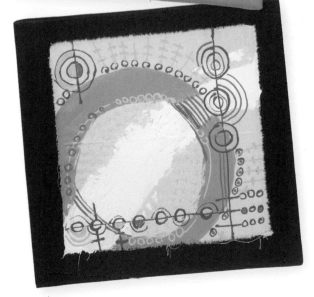

MIXED-MEDIA BIRTHDAY BOOK

A creative way to celebrate a special occasion.

beryl taylor

Created from shipping tags that can be picked up at your local office supply store, this little book makes excellent use of ordinary objects and leftover snips from previous projects. Each tag is decorated on one side then glued to its mate to make back-to-back pages that are bound together with sari silk ribbon. I made this book as a birthday gift for a friend. You can customize your book to tell a personal story for any occasion.

These instructions are intended as guidelines. Some of these techniques and materials may be new to you. Working in this small size with inexpensive materials can give you the freedom to experiment and become more comfortable with these processes.

Make this project personal by adding your own thoughts, words, fibers, and colors.

Mixed-Media Birthday Book
2½" × 5" (6.5 cm × 12.5 cm)

CONSTRUCTION

- Shipping tags, 2½" × 5" (6.5 cm × 12.5 cm) (available at office supply stores)
- Sari silk ribbon, 1 yard (0.9 m)
- Metal finials, 4
- Hole punch
- Low-odor glue

EMBELLISHMENTS

- Small pieces of sheers, silk organza, and lightweight fabrics
- Hand-printed fabric (I printed fabric using a Gelli Arts Printing Plate.)
- Muslin
- Deli paper, 2½" × 5" (6.5 cm × 12.5 cm) (Deli paper is translucent, very thin, strong, and inexpensive.)
- Pages from an old book
- Small silk or paper flower
- Buttons
- Acrylic paints, assorted colors plus gold metallic
- Inks (I used Liquitex Professional Acrylic Ink.)
- Thread (optional)
- Modeling paste
- Small paintbrush
- Rubber stamps (I used "Happy Birthday" and stamps with numbers.)
- Stencils

Make the Pages

Before you begin, spend a few moments thinking through the message you want to convey—is this a birthday celebration, anniversary, or graduation? Jot down a few images or phrases that would work with your theme.

1. For the cover of this book, I used wrinkled deli paper to add texture to the page, then added some stars made with modeling paste and a small stencil. Paint and inks add the color and shine. To state the theme, I stamped the birthday message on muslin and stitched it directly onto the shipping tag.

2. On some of the book pages, I simply added color and texture to continue the theme. I printed a series of numbers to reflect the counting that is usually done for birthday celebrations, but I also added in drawings of local plants and flowers and even small physical artifacts to add interest and to make this book more personal.

3. This is the perfect project to use small pieces of special fabric—even a square inch (2.5 cm) of hand-dyed cotton can make a statement.

4. Embellishments do not need to be perfectly flat. Small beads, silk or paper flowers, or other ephemera can be incorporated into the designs.

5. You may want your book to tell a story, in which case you'll want to arrange the pages in a specific order.

6. When you have all your pages complete, trim the fabric or paper collage pieces even with the edges of the tags. Glue the pages together back to back. Putting a little weight—such as a small book or food tin—on the page will help give the pages a good cohesion. Give the glue plenty of time to dry.

7. To finish the pages, edgestitch the perimeter of the pages, if desired. This is a great place for variegated thread. Paint the edges with gold paint.

8. Follow the Assembly Instructions to complete your book.

Methods

Here are several of the techniques that I used to make my Birthday Book. Most of these processes allow for some spontaneity and serendipity—so relax and enjoy!

Wrinkled Deli Paper With Raised Stencils

1. Paint a sheet of deli paper with acrylic paint that has been diluted with water.

2. Spray the paper randomly with Liquitex ink. The paper will wrinkle as it dries.

3. When the paper has dried, place a stencil over it and apply a light coat of modeling paste with a spatula. Remove the stencil.

4. Paint the background with diluted paints.

5. Paint the dried modeling paste with gold acrylic.

6. Glue the decorated deli paper to a shipping tag and trim to size.

| TIP: *You can use this method with organza instead of paper, but you will not be able to paint the background. Painting the shipping tag or layering the organza over colorful fabric will add some sizzle.*

Stamped Muslin

1. Paint a strip of muslin with acrylic paint.

2. Stamp your message on the muslin and add some painted or hand-stitched highlights.

3. Machine stitch along both edges for texture.

4. Glue the strip around the tag.

DIY Fabric Paper

1. Saturate a piece of muslin with a mixture of 1 part glue to 4 parts water. Cover the fabric with scrunched tissue paper.

2. Paint and let dry.

3. Stamp, draw, or embellish the fabric paper, then glue it to a tag.

Stitched Illustrations

1. Paint a piece of paper.

2. Draw on the painted paper and place it on a piece of muslin.

| TIP: *If you are not much of an illustrator, trace a copyright-free drawing.*

3. Machine stitch the outline of the illustration.

| NOTE: *Machine stitching on paper will dull the needle.*

4. Paint inside the stitched lines.

5. Glue the decorated paper panel to the tag and trim to size.

Fabric or Fabric/Paper Layering

1. Apply 2 strips of fabric to the tag, layering them slightly.

2. Hand- or machine stitch the edges and use the layered fabric as a background for other processes, or:

3. Glue a strip of type from a book page or a decorative fabric print to the tag and glue a strip of silk organza on top.

Assembly Instructions

1. To make a template for the holes, on a blank tag measure and mark a line ½" (1.3 cm) in from the spine. On this line, mark 1½" (3.8 cm) from the top of the tag and 1¼" (3.2 cm) up from the bottom. Punch holes at each intersection.

2. Place the template on each page and mark for the holes. With an awl or hole punch, make 2 holes on each tag.

3. Thread sari silk through the holes and tie loosely. Add metal finials to the silk ends.

GENERAL TIPS

- Handstitch buttons to a fabric strip. Glue and then machine stitch strips of fabric to the tag.

- Let paint, inks, and other mediums dry thoroughly before proceeding to the next step.

- Tear some fabrics—the hand-torn edges can look so beautiful—and cut others into strips and rectangles slightly bigger than the shipping tags.

CLOCKWISE FROM LEFT:

Painted deli paper, stamped muslin, and wrinkled deli paper with raised stencils

PLAYING WITH METAL LEAF ON FABRIC

Add texture and shine with thin sheets of metal.

ana buzzalino

One of my favorite new techniques is metal leafing. I started to experiment with it on fabric, as I wanted to see what the difference would be between metal leafing, foiling, and metallic painting.

The term "metal leaf" is used for thin sheets of metal of any color that do not contain any real gold. "Gold leaf" is genuine gold that has been hammered into thin sheets. It is available in a wide variety of karats and shades. The most commonly used is 22-karat yellow gold. In my work, I use imitation gold metal leaf as real gold leaf is quite expensive.

Come Let Us Plant an Apple Tree (detail)

MATERIALS

- Fabric of your choice
- Soft gel medium (I use Golden Gel Mediums.)
- Paint brush for applying gel medium (I use a foam brush.)
- Soft brush for burnishing
- Metal leaf adhesive
- Metal leaf sealant
- Container for water to clean brushes
- Plastic to cover the work surface

OPTIONAL

- Masking tape or painter's tape
- Freezer paper to create a stencil

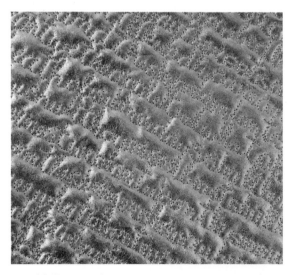

Metal foiling sample

Using Metal Leaf on Fabric

1. Cover your work surface with plastic. To prevent the metal leaf from being disturbed by air movement, make sure the windows are closed and fans are turned off. Always clean your brushes with the recommended cleaner immediately after use.

2. Metal leaf requires adhesive (or sizing) to adhere to the fabric. Because fabric is porous, I found that it absorbed the sizing and dried too quickly, without leaving enough for the metal leaf to adhere to. To offset that, seal the area where you are going to apply the metal leaf by first painting it with gel medium. Let dry thoroughly.

| NOTE: *If you want a definitive shape, delineate it with masking tape or make a stencil with freezer paper. Paint inside the area. Do not peel the masking tape/freezer paper until the end* (**FIGURE 1**).

3. Once the gel medium is dry, repaint the area with metal leaf sizing. Let it dry until tacky to the touch.

4. Open the package of gold leaf carefully. Lift one sheet at a time and place the gold leaf over the sizing.

5. Burnish with a soft brush.

| NOTE: *Keep small, leftover pieces for future use.*

6. If you don't get the entire area covered on the first pass, reapply the sizing, let dry, and reapply the metal leaf.

7. Once the area is covered, coat with a layer of sealer to prevent tarnishing.

| NOTE: *Imitation metal leaf will discolor in time, even when sealed. If you require archival longevity, consider using real gold leaf, which will not tarnish.*

FIG. 1

Untitled • 10½" × 8" (26.5 cm × 20.5 cm) (with metal leaf)

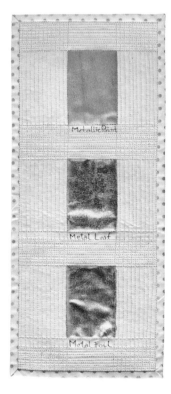

Metal Leaf, Foil, and Metallic Paint: What's the Difference?

Metal leaf, also called gold leaf (or silver, or copper, for example), comes in very fine sheets separated by paper. The sheets are very delicate and fall apart easily when applied to a surface. This is the effect that I prefer—the less-than-perfect application. Metal leaf is a messier process than foiling, where no pieces of the metal are left to fly around. Fabric that has metal leaf applied to it cannot be washed without damaging the metal leaf. The artwork in this article is meant for display only.

Foil is a high gloss Mylar that is covered with clear backing that peels away when heat is applied. Foil looks similar to metal leaf but is easier to apply and less expensive.

Both metal leaf and foil need a special glue to be applied to the surface. Foil can also be adhered using a fusible web such as Wonder-Under or Mistyfuse.

Metallic paint adds shimmer and sparkle in paint form, although paints do not have the rich metallic look of gold leaf. Metallic paint is the right choice for functional pieces that will be laundered.

CHAPTER **3**

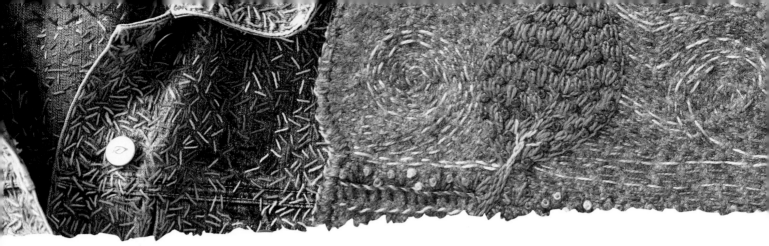

TAKE A *break!*

HAND STITCHING
WITH STYLE

"delicate remnants"
2014
leslie tucker jenison

SWEET LITTLE SOMETHINGS

A mixed-media take-along project for art on the go.

leslie tucker jenison

We artists are always fiddling with something—our hands need to be busy! Like me, you may need something artistic to do when you travel. "Sweet little somethings" are small collaged bits of cloth, paper, and trim that are stitched together by machine, by hand, or both. They are perfect to take when traveling or anywhere you might have a time to do a bit of stitchery.

I carry two small plastic zipper bags of art supplies when I travel. One contains my tiny watercolor set, a small sketchbook, a pen, a brush, watercolor postcards, and stamps. The other bag contains ingredients for my "sweet little somethings," including funky pieces of cloth—such as silk organza, vintage kimono silk, and leftovers from printing or dyeing projects—a few large-eye needles, some embroidery thread, and a small pair of TSA-friendly scissors. I think of these bags as a grown-up version of those "goodie packs" I parceled out to my young kids to keep them busy in a car or plane.

I was reawakened to the joy of hand stitching several years ago while attending a workshop with Mary Ruth Smith, a marvelous embroiderer who chairs the fiber department at Baylor University. I was further inspired last spring during a workshop with Cas Holmes, who adds to her own work with found cloth and trim, vintage handkerchiefs, and more. Although their work is quite different in approach and appearance, these artists share a love of spontaneous embroidery work that has impacted my own point of view.

MATERIALS

- Small pieces of cloth, paper, and trim (This project is an excellent way to use remnants. Consider including sheers, art paper, and ephemera.)

- Water-soluble stabilizer

- Embroidery threads

- Monofilament thread

- Embroidery needle

- Scissors

- Warm water and container to dissolve the stabilizer

OPTIONAL

- Buttons, beads, or other embellishments

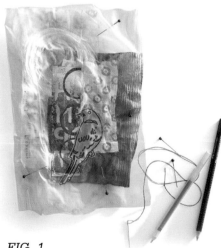

FIG. 1

Getting Started

These "somethings" have no lofty purpose beyond pleasing me as I create them. Truly, it is the process, not the product, that most delights me. Some of these works may become part of a larger piece, but that is not my purpose. I simply appreciate their nonprecious nature.

Quite frequently the bits of cloth combine with some travel ephemera, which I may attach to my sketchbook. The same is true of my travel paper collages. I frequently mail them to my home—a lovely reminder of the trip when I find them in my mailbox!

While many of these constructions are set aside and never finished, others become little compositions that are charming mounted on a piece of watercolor paper and framed.

These "sweet little somethings" are a form of meditation, a slowing down, a mindful pursuit of the rhythm that is stitching.

Making "Sweet Little Somethings"

1. Arrange small pieces of cloth, paper, and bits of trim to create a collage for a base.

2. Before you travel, sandwich the collage between 2 sheets of water-soluble stabilizer and pin lightly. Machine stitch the layers in place using monofilament thread **(FIGURE 1)**.

3. Remove the water-soluble stabilizer by immersing the stitched collage in warm water and gently rubbing the stabilizer.

| **TIP:** *It is sometimes necessary to rinse more than once to fully remove the gelatin product.*

4. Place the collage on a flat surface to dry.

5. Once dry, this collage may be further stitched by hand or embellished with buttons, beads, and other ephemera.

Displaying Your Creations

When finished, these small "somethings" are lovely framed or mounted on paper. I like to mount the collages by stitching them onto a backing—a small stitch with monofilament thread in each corner works well.

STITCHING THE SKETCHBOOK

Turning line drawings into fiber art.

susan brubaker knapp

In the past three years, I've been working to improve my sketching ability. While I've sketched off and on since I was little, I've never been disciplined about it and never thought my drawings were particularly good. But practice has made a difference. I'm now at the point that I love to sketch, and I am quite proud of some of my work.

As I started feeling better about what I was sketching, I also started wondering: How could I make this into fiber art? Nothing against paper, but it is not my primary medium. And I wondered if I worked from my sketches, rather than from photos as I usually do, whether it might take my work in a different direction.

It turned out to do exactly that. Not only do the new pieces exhibit a different style than my usual work, they also required me to work with new techniques that have helped me stretch as an artist.

I dedicated one sketchbook to simple line drawings. In this sketchbook, I forced myself to forgo my usual pencil lines first—and use only the ink. These sketches have a much freer, whimsical feel to them than my other sketching style. I found that I really enjoyed making these fast sketches of things from both my home environment and my travels.

Sketches of my sewing scissors were the inspiration for a quilt titled Never Enough, and inspired designs for an embroidered denim jacket and apron.

MATERIALS

- Embroidery needle with a large eye
- Perle cotton, size 5
- Lightbox (or bright window)

FOR THE QUILT

- Fabric, various pieces for quilt top and backing
- PFD (prepared-for-dyeing) white fabric (Pimatex PFD by Robert Kaufman is my go-to fabric for wholecloth painting. It is tightly woven with a high thread count which makes it ideal for tracing.)
- Firm stabilizer (I use Pellon 910 interfacing or Heavy Weight Shaping Aid.)
- Low-loft batting, cut to size
- Fabric paint (I use PROfab Textile Paints by ProChemical & Dye.)
- Aurifil 50-weight Cotton Mako thread
- Fine ink pens, such as Pigma Micron pens (These pens bleed less than others, even when paint hits the lines, are acid free, and come in varied thicknesses.)
- Fine-tip permanent marker (I use an Ultra Fine Point Sharpie.)

Embroidered Denim Jacket

When I travel to teach, I love to take something with me to work on while sitting in airports, on planes, and in hotel rooms. I came up with this jacket idea when I realized it would be great to have a project to work on—that I could also wear when I travel. Embroidering a denim jacket fit the bill (be sure to check TSA regulations before packing your bags). I could stitch on it to keep my blood pressure down during stressful air travel, and then put it on when I got chilly.

I purchased a jeans jacket made from cotton with a bit of spandex for $3 at a local thrift shop. The cotton/spandex fabric made it easy to stitch; 100% cotton denim can be tiring to embroider. Lightweight cotton canvas is also fun to stitch.

The first step was to transfer some of my simple line drawings of sewing items—scissors, thread spools, a tape measure, and a pincushion—onto the jacket.

After enlarging my sketches to the sizes I needed using a photocopier, I put them on my lightbox and positioned the jacket on top. In places that I couldn't see through the denim, I cut out the sketches, put them on top of the jacket, and traced around them.

Using perle cotton—both hand-dyed and straight from the spool—and an embroidery needle with a large eye, I stitched white lines around the sketched items in a running stitch with only a tiny space between each stitch. Then I filled in around

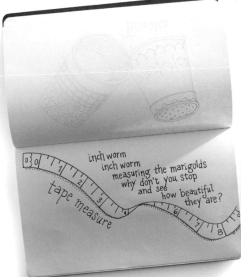

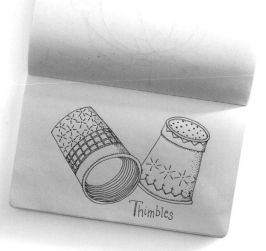

"
These sketches have a much freer,
whimsical feel to them than
my other sketching style.
"

the items with a stitch I call "chicken scratch" (see The Versatile Chicken-Scratch Stitch sidebar). The only areas that require extra care are the pockets (don't stitch them shut!) and the collar, cuffs, and bottom of the jacket (don't let knots and trailing bits of perle cotton hang out).

Although I'm not quite done with the jacket, I've been wearing it every step of the way.

Lenten Rose Quilt

This quilt started with a sketch of a flower with a lot of cross-hatching in the background (**FIGURE 1**). I enlarged a black ink drawing, and traced it onto white PFD fabric using a Pigma Micron pen. I painted it with PROfab Transparent Textile Paints from ProChemical & Dye. When dry, I layered it with batting and backing fabric, and quilted around the details with black, 50-weight thread. I also stitched in the negative areas around the flower at different angles, to emulate the cross-hatching I love to use in my sketches (**FIGURE 2**).

I used a bit of pale purple thread to lightly quilt some details on the petals. Since I usually paint for realism, this piece was a bit of a stretch for me. I worked more quickly than usual, and was pleased by its more spontaneous style.

FIG. 1

FIG. 2

"Making this art apron has provided me with hours of pleasure and makes me happy every time I wear it."

Pincushion

THE VERSATILE CHICKEN-SCRATCH STITCH

Having a piece of handwork to pick up when I have a bit of free time is something I've come to enjoy. And when I don't have to wait until it's finished to enjoy wearing it, it's even better! That's the beauty of my chicken-scratch stitches (which are just short stitches placed at random). As soon as one motif is finished, start wearing your project—then just add more images and chicken scratches whenever you have a few moments or want to unwind.

ON HAND STITCHING

Thoughts on making your mark with needle and thread.

lorie mcCown

I started my artist's way as a painter. Well, to be quite honest, I started as a collage artist, cutting up old Christmas and birthday cards to glue onto pieces of cardboard. I suppose that was a big clue that throughout my life—as an art student and as a professional artist—I would always be looking for and finding ways to recycle materials and use my hands to make things.

My first foray into the quilting world was innocent enough—I decided to make my newborn son a baby quilt. I had a garment sewing background and could read a pattern so I bought a commercial pattern and made my son a quilt. Even at that nascent stage, I wished to infuse that handmade object with my personal touch. I hand-embroidered his name, birthdate, and other information onto that quilt.

The simple act of needle pulling thread is a personal and intimate way of making your mark. Handwork is always my default method of making textile art.

Throughout the 1970s and 1980s I was always making. I enjoyed the slow rhythm of hand stitching, whether it was the needlepoint craze of the 1970s or embellishing clothing with lace and stitch, I was always willing to try it out. It was a natural evolution that my art quilts would include handwork.

Invisible Epiphanies (detail)

I am always looking for the artists' "hand" in their artwork. The sketchiness or the marks made by hand are indications of the time and effort put into a piece of art. The stitches in a quilt are very much the same. I'm looking to honor the traditional "women's work" of the humble stitch. I very much enjoy incorporating this into a contemporary statement in cloth and thread.

For the last few years, I have worked with recycled materials and I rarely buy new fabric anymore. There is just so much available for me to choose from, and I have a real love for old, mended, and worn-out fabrics and textiles. In fact, I usually draw extra meaning from those very materials for my work.

I keep all my tools and materials simple. I love the direct application of marks and eschew methods that distance rather than draw me closer to my work. I use embroidery floss, usually 2–3 strands, to do the stitching. I do all the handwork with a thimble. I pin most of my layers together; it's a very expedient way to work.

TOP TO BOTTOM:

Generations • 20" × 21" (51 cm × 53.5 cm)
Two Sisters • 22" (56 cm) square

ITEMS I ALWAYS HAVE ON HAND

- **BASE CLOTH:** Choose something easy to needle. Bed linens and batik fabrics are often very tightly woven so your fingers may get tired or sore. I've been working in long panels lately, so this usually determines the size of the piece.

- **COMPLEMENTARY FABRICS:** I like having many different textiles or fabrics available. I love recycled household textiles, tea towels, and even children's clothing. If you want to be creative, this is the place to let loose. Check your old trims, lace, and doilies. Sheer and gauzy fabrics are a big favorite of mine, too. Maybe now is the time to use old Aunt Enid's gloves in a project.

- **EMBROIDERY FLOSS:** I usually use 2–3 strands but I get creative here, too. Try threading a needle with 2 different-colored threads or a variegated variety. Think about featuring certain stitches.

- **LARGE-EYED EMBROIDERY NEEDLES:** I like John James of England needles. I like the large eyes because they are easier to see and thread.

- **THIMBLE:** This is optional but I'm a thimble wearer. I have a nice brass one I treasure.

Before you begin a project, start by just thinking. What matters to you? What is it that makes you want to take up needle and thread? What items would you like to use to convey your message? Take a bit of time to think these ideas over. Make notes in a notebook or sketchbook, and let them simmer a bit.

Start with a small sketch or design idea. Work with the fabrics you have. Don't fight them. Remember to respect the integrity of the cloth. Really think about the history of the materials you are using to create your work. Take it seriously, and think about what it means to you.

By starting with a base cloth, the size of your piece will be predetermined, more or less. It's your canvas. Start layering fabrics on to it. Don't forget to look at the reverse side, too. This can wield some interesting color or texture.

Generally, work large to small. Layer the larger pieces of textile followed by the smaller and pin them in place. Step back and assess your composition. You can always move things around before you stitch them down.

As you stitch the pieces down, try different stitches. A simple running stitch gives a linear, traveling effect. A buttonhole or blanket stitch can be effective for added textures. Experiment with different stitches. You will find a visual vocabulary that you like. Use that to your advantage. It's what makes the piece your own. As you get the rhythm of hand stitching, you will find you gravitate to certain stitches.

Continue layering fabrics and textiles. In this way, you make a rich, interesting composition. Consider cutting apart larger pieces and using them in several parts of the composition. Gloves can be deconstructed or used whole. The same for dresses, socks, or shirts—use them whole or in parts. Try to think creatively. Hand stitching and embroidery can really add life to a piece and create your own personal mark. Let your needle and your imagination travel across your work.

Hand stitching can also be an effective finishing on a piece. A blanket stitch edging is a very textural way to bind a quilt and is an alternative to a traditional binding. Or, consider leaving a raw or frayed edge. It's a soft way to end the piece.

Look for ways to increase your stitch vocabulary and use handwork in your quilts. It's a good way to take your work to a very personal level.

ABOVE RIGHT:

Generations (detail)

FABRIC CHOICES

- When choosing fabrics, I am very receptive. I love the unconventional and unexpected. Really try to open your mind about what you want your piece to be about. This is not technique-driven as much as concept-driven.

- If you are using old clothes, don't get too crazy about spots or stains. The fabrics have lived a life; let your piece be about that. In this way you elevate your pieces to art, art that connects with you and others. Frayed edges, ripped patches, and 'mended' spots are all interesting elements to include.

FREE-STITCHED EMBROIDERIES

Create small-scale drawings with thread.

laura wasilowski

Densely hand-stitched, these small vignettes of everyday life are
created without a drawing or pattern. They are embroidered with
a variety of different cotton threads and stitched on a solid-colored
wool fabric. The vignettes are rich in color, varied in texture, and
reflect the hand of the maker. Enjoy the slow, thoughtful tempo
of making intimate art work.

CLOCKWISE FROM LEFT:

Embroidered Pear (detail) • 5" x 6½" (12.5 cm × 16.5 cm)
Embroidered Landscape #2 • 5" × 5½" (12.5 cm × 14 cm)
Embroidered Plum • 4" × 5½" (10 cm × 14 cm)

MATERIALS

- Felted wool fabric, approximately 6" × 7" (15 cm × 18 cm)
- Perle cotton embroidery threads, sizes 5, 8, and 12 in a variety of colors
- Embroidery needles
  – size 3 for size 5 thread
  – size 3 or 4 for size 8 thread
  – size 5 or 7 for size 12 thread

Start Stitching

1. Select a shape for the design. Shapes should be simple with lots of open areas for embroidery.

2. Using size 5 thread, create an outline of the design shape on the wool (**FIGURE 1**). I don't mark my fabric first. These long running stitches work best for drawing the outline shape and will be removed after the shape is filled in with embroidery stitches.

| NOTE: *There is no need for a pattern. If the stitched shape is not to your liking, just pull the thread out and start over.*

3. Use the size 8 and 12 embroidery threads to develop 4–6 embroidery stitch combinations or motifs that can be repeated within the shape. Make small patches of the stitch combinations (less than 1" [2.5 cm] square) and fill in the shape. The patches may be square, curved, or unevenly shaped. Refer to the finished sample for suggestions.

4. After the inside of the shape is embroidered, remove the size 5 outlining thread.

5. Place an outline or stem stitch around the shape using the size 8 embroidery thread (**FIGURE 2**).

6. Create a background motif with stitches like the *running stitch* or *cross stitch* filled with *French knots*.

7. Finish the edge of the wool with a *blanket stitch*.

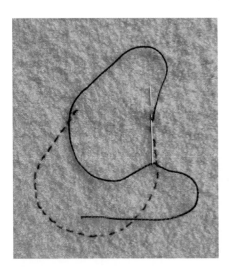

FIG. 1

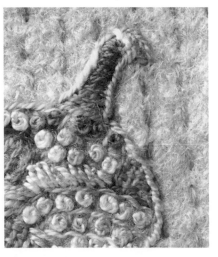

FIG. 2

FIG. 3

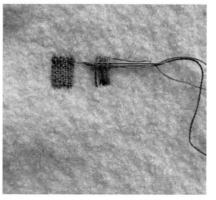

FIG. 4

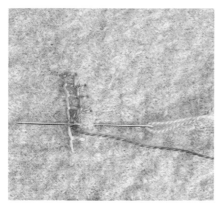

FIG. 5

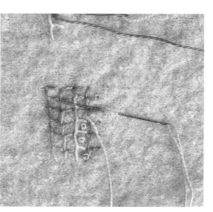

FIG. 6

FIG. 7

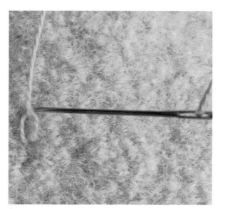

FIG. 8

FIG. 9

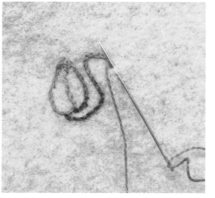

FIG. 10

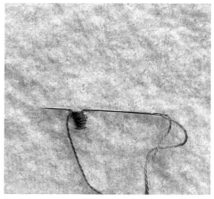

FIG. 11

STITCH TALK

Common embroidery stitches used in combination or by themselves make lovely fillers. For more stitches, consult an embroidery reference book or be creative and create your own motifs.

NEEDLE WEAVING:

Needle weaving creates a tiny patch of colored fabric **(FIGURES 3 & 4)**.

BLANKET STITCH:

Two rows of blanket stitch create a box shape that can be further embellished with French knots **(FIGURES 5 & 6)**.

LAZY DAISY STITCH:

Rows of lazy daisy stitches can be further enhanced with back stitches **(FIGURES 7–9)**.

STEM STITCH:

Stem stitches or outline stitches are perfect for making loops, parallel lines, and outlining other motifs **(FIGURE 10)**.

SATIN STITCH:

Combine rows of satin stitches with a dividing line of straight stitches for contrast **(FIGURE 11)**.

INTUITIVE HAND STITCHING

Ignite your creativity with unexpected art.

rita summers

My textile pieces often include recycled materials. Fabric and buttons from cast-off clothing, scraps, leftover thread, and other discards are hoarded until I find just the right place for them. I experiment with packaging materials, used tea bags, found objects, and fabric scraps. I have a deep, almost subconscious desire to find usefulness and beauty in what is perceived as waste.

This wall hanging (see detail at right) is part of an ongoing body of work I call "Earthsongs." In this series, I allow myself to indulge in techniques that could be seen as subversive. I embrace decay, allow frayed edges, and often tear fabric instead of cutting it. I tie knots in the fabric, let loose threads hang down, and permit thread knots to show on the front of my work. I simplify. I include broken, rusty, and discarded items other people throw out. I allow the fabric and materials to speak for themselves and they speak of the things that are in my mind. Somehow these things are transferred into my work.

My method of creating is usually done without much planning. I start with an idea rather than a complete design and allow my creativity to flow. Creating a piece entirely by hand is satisfying and connects me to the past. When you operate this way, wonderful and unexpected things happen. Thoughts, feelings, memory, images, and words rise to the surface and are "written" in your creations.

Lost/Found (detail)

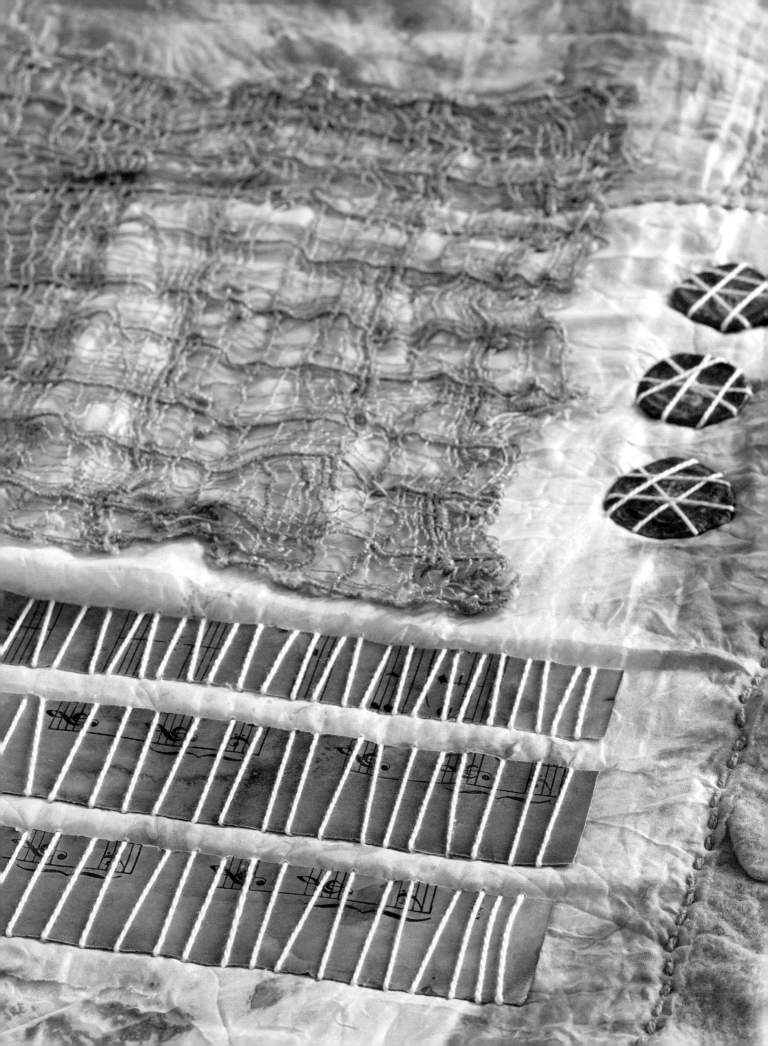

MATERIALS

- Dyed or rusted batting (wool or cotton)

- Dyed or rusted fabrics of various weights and transparencies for layering (I use several types of silk and lightweight home décor fabric.)

- Old sheet music or other found papers

- Found objects such as rusty bottle caps, nails, and the metal clips from broken clothespins (see Gathering Materials for Your Own Earthsong Quilt)

- Perle cotton

- Handsewing needle

- Scissors

- Digital camera

OPTIONAL

- Painter's or masking tape

- Crochet motifs to use as appliqué, purchased or handmade

DYEING & RUSTING FABRIC AND PAPER

There are many dyeing and rusting products and recipes. The key to finding which works best for you is experimentation. I use natural dyes made from plants in my garden, commercial dyes, and/or rusting solutions for much of my work. I often do this in advance and in bulk, which gives me a selection of fabrics and papers to play with when I want to begin a new project.

Start Exploring

My aim is to explore a variety of ideas, techniques, and influences to create a visual expression of my emotional response to life and the world around me. I urge you to work this way, too. You will find that your creations will be unique—after all, your responses, your world, your experiences, and your reactions are your own!

Most importantly, enjoy yourself, relax, and go with the flow. Let the materials and the processes show you what they want you to do. Work intuitively—and discover the unexpected.

1. Determine the size of the artwork you want to make. Cut or tear a piece of batting slightly larger than the finished size of your piece.

2. Select fabrics, papers, found objects, and threads you want to use on your piece. Cut or tear the fabrics and papers to size.

3. Arrange the collage elements on the batting in layers in a way that is pleasing to you. Allow yourself to play without too many preconceived ideas about the end product.

4. Arrange the found objects on your work. Try not to be too symmetrical. Trust your eye to assess the balance and composition of your work as you progress. Move things around if they don't look right or replace items. Partially overlap some layers.

5. When you are happy with your design, take a photograph with a digital camera so you can remember where all of the components should be placed.

6. Decide which items or layers need to be stitched down first, then remove everything else. Keep the photograph close by to remind you how it all goes back together.

7. Start sewing the items down to the batting by hand, one at a time. Try out different stitches and use a variety of thread colors. I like to keep this type of work quite simple, so I mainly use a running stitch, seed stitch, cross stitch, and fly stitch. Leave knots and thread ends exposed if this is the effect you want.

8. Papers and found objects can be sewn to the background by wrapping stitches around them. This is especially useful if you don't want puncture marks in your papers, or if your found objects don't have convenient holes in them.

9. After everything is attached, start to fill in some of the blank areas of fabric with more stitching. In my wall hanging, I used a running stitch to add texture to the background.

10. Tear the bottom edge of the wall hanging into strips and knot them randomly. Then stitch a torn fabric rod pocket onto the back top edge, and label your work.

| **TIP:** *I prefer to stitch freehand when I do this kind of work. However, painter's or masking tape is a good way to keep your lines straight if you prefer. It can be used a number of times, but don't leave it on for too long or it will leave a sticky residue.*

GATHERING MATERIALS FOR YOUR OWN EARTHSONG QUILT

FOUND OBJECTS: These can be found in the most unexpected places. I have tins full of broken glass, rusty bottle caps, old nails, keys, buttons, and anything else I think I might use one day.

THREADS: Experiment with different threads such as wool, perle cotton, embroidery floss, string, or even thin wire.

STITCHES: Play with a variety of embroidery stitches to see what suits your work. You could even use this project as a unique stitch sampler.

PAPERS: I use lots of different paper ephemera in my work. Often, the papers have been dyed or rusted first, then covered with a thin layer of shellac before attaching them to the fabric.

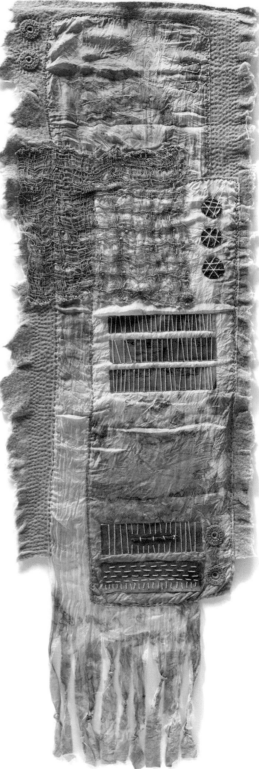

lost/found
43½" × 15" (110.5 cm × 38 cm)
"art is like breathing to me
life and thoughts impressed
on paper, cloth, the air
fleeting sounds and images
captured before they escape forever"
—Rita Summers

THE SEED STITCH

An in-depth look at one of the most versatile hand-stitching techniques.

jane dávila

Stitching is what sets fiber art and quilts apart from other art forms such as painting, sculpture, or drawing. As the initial layers of colors and forms are completed, an entirely new layer of design comes into play when stitches are added. Stitch and the paths that are created when the thread travels across the surface are powerful tools in a fiber artist's toolbox. Through them we have the ability to direct a viewer's eye, to create a compelling focal point, to draw attention toward or deflect attention from a particular element or space on a piece, and to create a texture that is at once visual and physical, that can be seen and felt.

The seed stitch, also known as a scratch stitch, chicken stitch, or rice stitch, is the workhorse of fiber art hand stitches. Artists love this stitch for a myriad of reasons: It is versatile, easy to master, and effective. The seed stitch can be used to connect areas across fabrics and shapes, to create both physical and visual texture for interest, to fill large areas quickly, and to add or influence the color of underlying fabrics. It can also be used to alter the scale or pattern of the work, to lead the viewer's eye along an intentional path of movement through a piece, to add emphasis to one or more specific areas, and to give the artist the opportunity to add an intuitive, organic, or seemingly unplanned element to a work.

The Army Wife: Home Fires (detail)

St. Pete Lace 13
15" (38 cm) square, Natalya Aikens

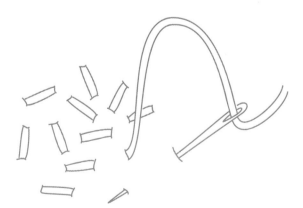

FIG. 1

The Seed Stitch

Seed stitches are short, straight stitches added in random directions to emulate the appearance of small seeds or grains of rice tossed onto a background. They are typically added once machine quilting has been completed so that the seed stitches are not quilted over, diluting their effect and flattening them. Stitches can vary by length, color, and choice of thread. Embroidery floss (any number of strands depending on the effect desired) is typically used for seed stitches, but other threads are just as beautiful.

Make the Stitch

Starting on the back of a piece, either bury the tail of the thread between the layers of fabric or use a small knot to secure the end. Come up through the front of the piece. Take a small stitch and repeat (**FIGURE 1**). Stitches can penetrate all the way to the back for maximum loft and texture, or travel within the top and batting for a flatter look. Stitches can be anywhere from ⅛–½" (3 mm–1.3 cm) in length or longer. For the characteristic "tossed seed" effect, add stitches in random directions, filling an area to your liking. See The Flip Side sidebar for options to consider while stitching. Finish by taking a backstitch on the reverse of the piece, tying a knot, or weaving the thread end between the layers of the front and back to hide it.

When to Seed Stitch

I asked four artists—Natalya Aikens, Deborah Boschert, Gerrie Congdon, and Kristin La Flamme—to share insight into how and when they use seed stitches in their work. Deborah especially loves variegated floss for seed stitch because, she says, "It's really effective for subtle color change across a broad area." Gerrie prefers hand-dyed threads and one of Natalya's favorites is a heavy silk thread.

Perle cotton or rayon, silk or linen floss, plain or variegated, matte or shiny threads all yield different results and can be combined for even more variety. In the piece *Seven Houses Five Trees*, Deborah created stitches with embroidery floss and layered them with larger stitches using regular sewing thread, noting "I love the contrast in the thickness of the floss and thread combined with the different stitch lengths."

Seed stitches can effectively fill areas of background or foreground for aggressive or quiet texture. Filling an area with seed stitches of differing color can change the way the viewer perceives the original, underlying color of the fabric or shape. Deploying seed stitch to form a visual bridge between

Seven Houses Five Trees
12" (30.5 cm) square
Deborah Boschert

10 WAYS TO USE THE SEED STITCH IN YOUR ART

1. Change the length of the seed stitches as you approach a focal point to create a sense of depth or perspective.

2. Vary the value of the colors of threads used for an ombré effect.

3. Arrange all of the stitches in the same direction for a strong path of movement.

4. Draw attention to a focal point by changing the thread color to a deeper, more saturated color as you near the area.

5. Create visual interest by using a pattern of stitches instead of a random design.

6. Pay attention to the spaces between the stitches for a thoughtful use of negative space.

7. Intersect design elements with seed stitches to tie them together visually.

8. Alter or influence the color of underlying fabrics by using a complementary or contrasting colored thread.

9. Draw attention to an area by altering the density or length of the stitches.

10. Consider using a double seed stitch—two close parallel stitches that look more like barley—or crossing the stitch for interest.

different elements or areas of the quilt is particularly useful. For example, Deborah names it one of her most versatile stitches, saying, "Seed stitch can be very effective in softening areas where the contrast between two fabrics might be visually distracting." Kristin uses seed stitch both to define an area, and to tie different areas together. In her art apron, *The Army Wife: Home Fires*, she used the seed stitch to blur the edges between collaged fabric elements, but she notes, "In other instances, I have defined the edge of a motif by using seed stitch quite densely, then fading to sparse stitches." Natalya has used seed stitch as a narrow border all the way around a piece, so it becomes a ghostly frame. Gerrie feels the organic look of seed stitching can add so much to an otherwise simple composition. "I love the idea of mark making with thread and it can be very effective for illustrating an element in the composition."

For Kristin, the best way to use seed stitch is as a blender. "I find that it visually supports other stitches and can even bring attention to them, yet it doesn't compete. It's also great for subtly (or not so subtly) modulating a background." She goes on, "I feel that I have more control over it than machine stitching and it offers more opportunities for variation in color and weight. It's faster and looser than say, French knots (which I also love a lot), and doesn't call as much attention to itself so it plays well with other stitches, fabrics, and styles." Natalya muses that she adds seed stitch "when I feel the piece needs something organic, something not very perfect."

Haiku: Forgotten Song—Shadow Beside
12" × 9" (30.5 cm × 23 cm)
Jane Dávila

The Zen of Hand Stitching

There is a Zen or meditative quality to the practice of adding hand stitching to fiber art. The slight, whispering rasp of the thread pulling through the fabric; the slow, thoughtful contemplation of each stitch's placement, length, and direction; the tactile pleasure of handling the chosen fabrics and threads; and the rhythm of your hands as the needle draws thread back and forth, up and down. Artists agree. Deborah explains, "It's meditative and easy, but not mindless. I do have to think just a little about the direction and length of each stitch, but that keeps me engaged. Hand embroidery always creates an intimate relationship between the cloth and the artist. I believe that shows in the finished product."

THE FLIP SIDE

Whether you choose to hide the knots and ends of the threads on the back of your work is a matter of personal choice and depends on the intended venue for showing your work. If your own comfort level demands that the back of your work be as tidy as the front, then by all means, hide and bury all tail ends of your threads. If you will be entering a piece in a show judged by "quilt show" rules, then the back needs to be as finished as the front, regardless of your comfort level. If, however, your piece will be entered in an art show where the back receives zero consideration, just make sure the work holds together and is soundly constructed.

The Army Wife: Home Fires
23" × 37" (58.5 cm × 94 cm)
Kristin La Flamme

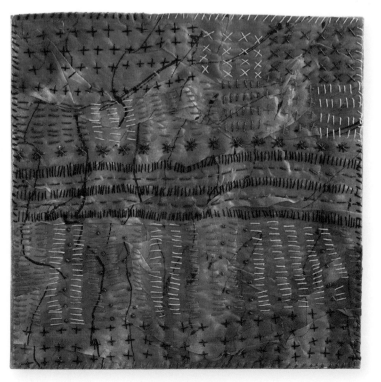

Fiesta • 12" (30.5 cm) square, Gerrie Congdon

CHAPTER 4

TAKE A *field trip*

SKETCHBOOK TO
ART QUILT

NOSTALGIA SERIES

Stitched sketches and ephemera in art quilts.

jane lafazio

I started this series of quilts after reading Cas Holmes' book, *The Found Object in Textile Art* (Interweave, 2010). I was so inspired by Cas's stitched sketches and the addition of paper and found items in her work.

In the past, before I owned a sewing machine, I used old letters in my hand-stitched organza quilts. I've also used some of the images from my sketchbook in my fiber art. And, in the last few months, I've been working on my free-motion machine stitching. So Cas Holmes' book spoke to all my interests, at just the right time, and started me creating what I call my "Nostalgia Series."

CLOCKWISE FROM TOP:

Zinnia
9½" × 13" (24 cm × 33 cm) • The pink zinnia is an image transfer onto a vintage cocktail napkin.

Thistle and Rose Hips
12" × 7" (30.5 cm × 18 cm)

Nostalgia Series
12" (30.5 cm) square • Part of an old postcard is caught in a free-motion stitched flower. This flower was tinted using water-soluble crayons, and French knots were stitched in the flower centers. Hand stitching was used to secure the edges of the postcard to the quilt.

high altitude egret
eh eventimies in
monotonous tempo,
aurtness, deep. As
no these troubled

MATERIALS

- Fabric
- Batting
- Sandwich wrap, deli paper, or tissue paper
- Pins
- Ephemera such as paper, ribbon, maps, and old letters
- Tulle
- Sewing machine with a free-motion foot
- Your own drawings (or images from decorative paper napkins, as Cas Holmes suggests)
- Fabric scraps such as silk organza, lace, cheesecloth, and recycled silk sari ribbon
- Embroidery thread and needle

OPTIONAL

- Grafix Dura-Lar Wet Media Film
- Soft gel medium
- Spoon (for burnishing)
- Water-soluble crayons

A cyanotype provided inspiration for the floral motifs in her Nostalgia Series.

Stitch a Drawing

1. Select a richly patterned fabric that sets the mood for your background. I used cloth I'd created by monoprinting with soy wax and fabric dyes.

2. Attach the batting to the back of the cloth as desired.

3. Select a drawing from your sketchbook, and scan it onto a piece of sandwich wrap or deli paper, or trace it onto a piece of tissue paper. I have used sketches, continuous line drawings, and even a cyanotype print for images. You can even experiment with image transfer (see Image Transfers).

4. Determine where you want your first stitched image to be on the front of your quilt and pin ephemera or sheer cloth in that spot. (When you sew from the back of the quilt, the stitching will catch the ephemera/sheer cloth on the front.)

5. Turn the quilt over and pin the paper drawing to the back of the quilt (on the batting).

6. Free-motion stitch from the back of the quilt, following the lines of your image. Tear away the excess paper, but don't worry about removing it; no one will see it. Your stitched design will be seen on the front of the quilt, and the stitching will have caught the bit of ephemera on the front.

7. Stitch one image at a time, overlapping the stitching and ephemera to create a layered surface design on the quilt.

8. Once the images are stitched with the ephemera in place, add tulle as a layer of subtle shading on areas of the quilt by pinning tulle to the top of the quilt. Machine stitch around the shape you want to cover with tulle, then using small scissors, cut away any excess tulle just outside the stitched line.

9. Add bits of fabric such as vintage lace and recycled sari ribbon.

10. Handstitch as desired around the paper, or in the body of the quilt, using a variety of colors of embroidery thread. I stitched French knots in the centers of the flowers.

Cocktail napkins can serve as an excellent design source for interesting motifs.

Image Transfers

I used a nifty product called Grafix Dura-Lar Wet Media Film to transfer an image of a pink zinnia onto a vintage cocktail napkin (see the Zinnia design). Follow these steps if you wish to do likewise.

1. Print your image onto the film using an inkjet printer. (It's best to use the printout immediately.)

2. Thinly spread soft gel medium over the surface of the fabric.

3. Place the film, printed side down, onto the wet gel, and burnish it.

4. Lift the film carefully and wash off the film immediately, as the film can be reused.

5. Let the fabric dry completely.

| **TIP:** *To enhance or slightly alter the color on the image transfer, use water-soluble crayons.*

TIP

The thread in the bobbin will show on the front of the quilt. I often select a bobbin thread color that will blend in with the background. Then I stitch again from the front of the quilt, with a black thread, so the stitched drawn lines are more visible. I do this because I'm a little nervous about my free-motion stitching, and doing it first in a neutral color helps get the drawing onto the cloth. Plus, stitching from the top refines the lines and gives it a nice sketchy quality.

ABOVE: *Two watercolors from Jane's journal.*

CREATE A CANVAS FOR COLOR

Make wholecloth designs using your sketchbook for inspiration.

jeannie palmer moore

This series of quilts was inspired by the sketchbook I kept while visiting the Gulf Coast of Louisiana and Mississippi. It's very important for me to always pack my sketchbook and markers. I don't plan out any designs for quilts while I'm traveling, but instead concentrate on sketching what interests me. Once I'm home, I'm able to design my quilts by referencing my drawings and photos.

I have recently been creating a canvas-type texture on muslin with spray gesso, and the grainy effect seems to work well when I'm transforming sketchbook designs to wholecloth quilts. Spray gesso dries quickly so you can start adding color in a few minutes, and the speckled spray of the gesso gives a rough surface for the color to stick to. I use water-soluble crayons, water-soluble ink pencils, and permanent markers in a wet-into-wet layering technique. Once I have created the background painting, I sometimes like to enlarge certain drawings from my sketchbook and make a freezer paper stencil for the gesso.

CLOCKWISE FROM TOP LEFT:

Fiddler Crab • 13" (33 cm) square
Mississippi Marshlands • 17" × 8" (43 cm × 20.5 cm)
Pelican Pier • 12" (30.5 cm) square

MATERIALS

- Muslin fabric
- Batting, backing fabric, and binding fabric
- Gesso spray (I use Krylon brand.)
- Water-soluble crayons
- Ink pencils (I use Derwent Inktense Watersoluble Ink Pencils.)
- Permanent, fine-line ink pens
- Masking tape
- Freezer paper
- Newspaper to cover your work area
- Watercolor paintbrush
- Water in a spray bottle
- Plexiglas or plastic surface
- Craft knife
- Iron and ironing surface
- Pressing cloth or parchment paper
- Sewing machine with free-motion stitching capabilities
- Sewing-machine thread in a variety of colors

Preparing the Cloth

1. Cut the muslin to your desired quilt size. Lay it on a newspaper-covered surface in a well-ventilated outside area.

2. Spray the gesso in light coats over the muslin. Not all areas of the fabric need to be covered.

3. Allow the fabric to dry for 15–20 minutes.

Adding Color

1. Place a piece of Plexiglas or a sheet of plastic on your work surface. Tape your prepared fabric to the plastic surface.

2. Transfer the outlines of a drawing from your sketchbook, or draw directly onto the fabric with a pencil.

3. Lightly spray the fabric with water, then start coloring with water-soluble crayons and ink pencils.

| **TIP:** *More water may be added if a less-defined look is desired. You may also want to let the fabric dry each time before you go back into areas to add more intense color with the crayons. Water-soluble ink pencils can be used while the fabric is still wet to create sharper lines.*

4. Once the fabric is dry, outline certain areas with permanent, fine-line ink pens.

Creating a Stencil for Gesso

1. Enlarge a drawing from your sketchbook and trace it in the center of a large piece of freezer paper. (The large area around your design will catch any overspray.)

2. Cut out your design carefully with a craft knife, preserving both the positive and negative areas.

3. Position and iron the positive piece of freezer paper (the solid white cutout) in place on your quilt (**FIGURE 1**).

4. Darken the outside edges of fabric around the freezer paper shape with crayons, blending the strokes into your design. (This is especially important if the background area is light, as it creates contrast to the white gesso you'll be spraying, but this step may be eliminated if the background area is dark enough.)

5. Position and iron the negative piece of freezer paper, registering it with the positive piece that is already in place (**FIGURE 2**). Carefully remove the positive piece of freezer paper.

FIG. 1

FIG. 2

6. Make sure the area of fabric around the negative piece is protected from any overspray. Spray the stencil with gesso in a well-ventilated outside area, spraying as many coats as necessary to achieve the desired white texture.

7. Carefully remove the freezer paper stencil; you can do so immediately if you like.

8. Allow the fabric to dry completely before ironing it with a pressing cloth.

Finishing

1. Create a quilt sandwich with the muslin top, batting, and backing fabric. Pin the layers in place, then add free-motion stitching.

2. Bind your quilt as desired.

SKETCHING WITH WATERCOLOR PAINTS

Inspiration for fiber art.

sue bleiweiss

Flip open my everyday sketchbook and you'll find pages filled with scribbles, lists, and drawings that are probably indecipherable to anyone but me. That was my preferred method of sketchbook keeping until I discovered watercolors a few years ago.

Using watercolors allows me to play with shape, line, composition, and color combinations. It's also a great way to nudge the muse awake when I'm not feeling particularly inspired or I'm in a creative slump. The watercolor paintings that I create are not intended to be finished works of art—they're the beginning steps I take when planning a piece of fiber art.

I prefer working with an inexpensive set of watercolor paint. The colors are bright and vivid and match the color palette of fabrics that I use in my quilts. I often use colored pencils in place of watercolor paints when I'm working outside or in a place where it's more convenient to work with pencils than with water.

Tutti Frutti Lane (detail)

Makes 4 coasters

- Watercolor paintings for inspiration
- Solid fabric scraps for each cup, approximately 4" (10 cm) square
- Black fabric, approximately 8" (20.5 cm) square
- Blue fabric for the background, (2) 21" (53.5 cm) squares and (4) 5" (12.5 cm) square
- Wool felt, 21" (53.5 cm) square
- Fusible web
- Quilting thread
- Black thread

Watercolor Paintings as Inspiration

The coffee cup paintings are a great example of how using watercolor sketches of a simple shape has influenced my quilt-making process. In this series, I limited my focus to the shape of the cup, and didn't worry about creating perfect paintings. The painted images became the inspiration for a large wall quilt, *Coffee Cups*, a series of small 8" (20.5 cm) square quilts (FIGURE 1), and coffee cup coasters. Because I made a variety of painted sketches in my sketchbook, I had a wide variety of inspiration for these pieces. And the color combinations I used in my original paintings had a big influence on the colors I eventually used in the finished fiber pieces.

My preferred method of translating my watercolor paintings to quilts is to use my own hand-dyed fabrics combined with fusible appliqué. I enjoy the process of creating an art quilt beginning with white fabric all the way through to creating the finished piece. But there are many techniques an artist could use to turn their paintings into a piece of fiber art. Explore one or all of these techniques in your own work!

FIG. 1

FIG. 2

Coordinating Coasters

The process I use to create the coasters that were inspired by my coffee cup watercolor paintings is simple and straightforward. Use it as a springboard for your own creative exploration.

1. Create a watercolor painting with a simple shape to use as inspiration (**FIGURE 2**).

2. Following the manufacturer's directions, iron a layer of fusible web onto the back of the fabrics you will be using in the project.

FIG. 3

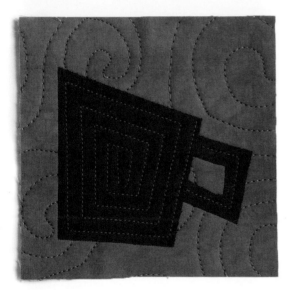

FIG. 4

FIG. 5

3. Fuse the large pieces of blue background fabric to the front and back of the wool felt, creating a 3-layer "sandwich." Quilt the sandwich as desired (**FIGURE 3**). I find it is much easier to quilt the piece at this point rather than after it has been cut to size and the imagery has been fused on top. Cut the quilted background into (4) 5" (12.5 cm) squares.

4. Using the painting as inspiration, free-cut the coffee cup and handle shapes from the scraps of solid fabrics and fuse them in place on the background squares. Add some quilting to the cup and handle if you wish (**FIGURE 4**).

5. Cut ⅛" (3 mm) wide strips from the black fabric and fuse them over the edges of the cup shape. Straight stitch over the edges with black thread.

6. Once all of the quilting is done, fuse a small 5" (12.5 cm) square of blue background fabric to the back of the coaster to hide all of the stitching.

7. Finish the edges with a zigzag stitch (**FIGURE 5**).

| **TIP:** *Rather than trying to cover the edges of the coaster using a satin stitch, make 2 or 3 passes around the edges with a zigzag set a little shorter than the sewing machine's default setting.*

MORE SKETCH INSPIRATION

- Logos from restaurants, wine bottles, museums, and stores you visit.

- If you find a fantastic restaurant, you might want to embroider their telephone number into your work.

- If you take public transit, stitch the line number.

- If you fly to get to your destination, stitch your flight number.

Coffee Cups
34" × 59" (86.5 cm × 150 cm)
Quilting by Kathy Perino

READY, SET, PAINT!

When working with watercolors it can be hard not to dip your paintbrush into every color on the palette. You will have more success if you set some limits.

- WORK IN A SERIES: Choose a single geometric shape such as a circle, square, or triangle, or you can try something with a touch more realism such as a leaf or flower petal. Explore the shape by making several paintings that are related but different. The object is not to recreate the perfect image, but to create a springboard of ideas to work from.

- LIMIT YOUR COLOR PALETTE: Create your paintings using just two colors plus black or white. If two colors is too limiting, then add a third color.

- WORK SMALL: I find it helpful to work with 6" (15 cm) squares of watercolor paper. This size gives me enough space to paint without being overwhelmed and I can move very quickly from one painting to the next without having to wait for the paint to dry. Once the paintings are dry, I either bind them into their own sketchbook or glue them onto a blank page.

STITCH JOURNALING

Capture memories with travel-inspired stitching.

melanie testa

I love travel—taking a trip to a new and undiscovered locale is invigorating and magical. Often, vacations are taken with loved ones and these trips become sparkling gems that we can look back upon to conjure up the fun and excitement of finding that awesome restaurant, exploring a great museum, or seeing that interesting (though odd) bit of graffiti. While a watercolorist might bring paper and paint to document such a trip, I like to document my journey through what I call "stitch journaling."

I use stitch and embroidery to interpret and engage with my surroundings. But since handwork, by its very nature, is a slow process, photography is an integral part of stitch journaling. Through my photos, I can look back to a specific moment of inspiration and resume stitching later that day or week. Usually when I embark on stitch journaling, I am committed to completing the item either while on the trip or just after returning home—my intention is to capture the spontaneity and verve of the experience.

My camera is an essential part of my ability to stitch on the go. I always carry a camera and take photos at every turn. Whenever I stop to examine something that might inspire me to stitch, out comes the camera. The zoom feature is a saving grace, allowing me to zoom in on a detail or remember a spelling.

FIG. 1

FIG. 2

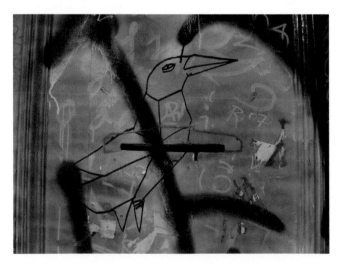

FIG. 3

Stitching Inspiration

By stitching our inspirations on fabric, we expand our memory of that original moment. As an example, take a look at this stone work outside a hotel in Bilboa, Spain (**FIGURE 1**). Just by looking at my stitched reminder, I remember the chill of morning air and the glossy wetness on the street as my husband and I headed out for breakfast. When traveling, remain on the lookout for patterns that can be easily interpreted in stitch.

I am often drawn to things that are much too complex to be interpreted in stitch. For example, I loved the Antoni Guadí mosaic tile work at Park Güell in Barcelona, but was I drawn to the color, the sheer volume of mosaics, or the chipped and cracked effect of the mosaic? In this case, it is best to identify what you are connecting with prior to stitching. I was fascinated by the broken and cracked nature of the mosaics and I also liked the round circles, so I took a photo of a simpler section of mosaic and worked from that (**FIGURE 2**). Once I identified the connection I felt to the imagery, I stitched a smattering of cracked and broken circles across the surface of my work.

Street art and graffiti are some of my favorite things to look for when traveling. Graffiti artists will often repetitively draw or "tag" the same image or word again and again. Repetition leads to an ease and confidence in a given subject. Graffiti artists generally need to work quickly while tagging in a recognizable style; because of this, the imagery they use will often have a finished, polished quality to it. The bird image seen here is one that I instantly fell in love with (**FIGURE 3**).

When I stumbled on this bit of graffiti (**FIGURE 4**), I was taken aback. It was painted on the wall using a roller—not marker or spray paint—and I estimate it was about 12 feet tall. This graffiti artist had both the time and audacity to complete this work in two colors. I connected with this imagery to such a degree that upon my return home, I promptly redesigned and cut a stencil for repeated use in several media, including stitch (**FIGURE 5**).

More often than not, I embroider using no marks or pre-drawn lines when I stitch journal. I accept the simplistic nature of my drawing and stitching skills and think this is part of the charm of journaling while using thread on cloth. Transferring ideas to your cloth is the most difficult part of stitching on the go.

I encourage you to trust yourself and simply stitch. If that makes you uncomfortable, use a mechanical pencil on lighter fabrics or a white pencil on dark fabrics. Mark the cloth lightly and faintly to ensure the stitching will cover each mark. Or simply embrace the aesthetic qualities of seeing pencil marks in your work!

FIG. 4

FIG. 5

When choosing fabrics to embroider, consider using solids or prints with simple backgrounds that will not compete with your hand-stitched marks. Audition thread choices by placing them atop your stitch work to help you decide if your design will benefit from high contrast or if a lighter, more integrated color will suit your idea better. Or use your clothing and fabric accessories as your canvas. The best thing about stitch journaling on my purses and clothing is that the memories of those trips comes flooding back each time I use the item.

I tend to gravitate to a few, well known and oft used embroidery stitches—backstitch, French knots, running stitch, fly stitch, lazy daisy— or simply stitch densely in an area for fill or texture. If you don't already have a set of "go to" stitches that you are comfortable with, leaf through an embroidery stitch dictionary and make a quick sampler of a few stitches that strike your fancy (**FIGURE 6**).

Of course, we need to take photos of our travels and the sights we see. This can be a great way to connect with loved ones to conjure the memories of that stellar vacation. But don't forget to use your artist's eye to discover inspiring designs. Capturing images with your camera and then interpreting them in stitch while sitting in a local coffee shop or restaurant will more deeply embed those same memories into your consciousness. Small details that might otherwise get lost in the passage of time remain clear and present to you because you took the time to stitch your memories.

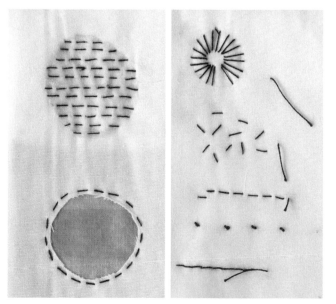

FIG. 6

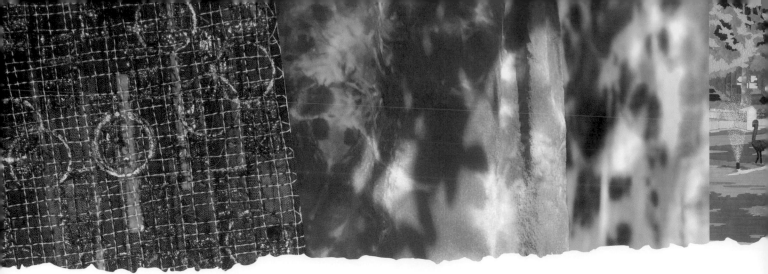

CHAPTER **5**

MAKE NEW *friends!*

GROUP PROJECTS FOR
ART QUILTERS

A PARTY TO DYE FOR

Tips for hosting an art gathering.

kristine lundblad

When I excitedly told my friends and family I was planning to host a dyeing party, they were puzzled. Why in the world would I be so excited about something to do with *dying* and what was there to party about? After I spelled it out and explained myself, I was met with relief but still a bit of confusion. How could that be a party?

Artists who dye their own fabric may think the same thing. After all, dyeing is a messy process and requires a lot of advance preparation. With just a little thoughtful planning, however, anyone can host a dyeing party. And who doesn't love an invitation to play in someone else's studio?

I asked for suggestions from a few fellow *Quilting Arts* contributors— April Sproule, Robin Ferrier, Carol Ludington, and Lynda Heines—who graciously offered thoughtful insights that made my party a success.

Photo Credit: Art Illman

THE INVITATION

I printed the invitations on plain paper, cut them to size, and sewed them onto fabric. There was so much information to pass on, I used several pages and folded the fabric, accordion-style, to fit into the envelopes. If your fabric seems limp, try some iron-on starch or sizing.

Be sure to include important information, such as:

- Detailed supply list
- Safety precautions
- What to wear

I also let them know what I was providing—which, besides supplies for the dyeing, included lunch while we were giving our fabric time to soak in the dye bath.

Know Your Guests

It is important to know the skill level of the people you are inviting. Are they experts or novices? The group of friends I invited had little dyeing experience so I needed to plan the day carefully, giving them advance warning on everything from what to wear to how to safely handle dyes.

If your guests don't sew or quilt, choose an easy project. April suggested silk scarves, which can be purchased hemmed and prepared for dyeing (PFD). Robin thought a grocery tote bag or set of cotton napkins would be fun and functional. Carol would encourage guests to bring worn table linens, pieces of lace, or crocheted doilies to dip in the dye pot, too. Robin took that idea a step further and suggested guests bring something other than cotton or silk—like cheesecloth, wood, an egg, paper, bamboo, or whatever—just for fun.

If your friends know their way around a dye pot, both Carol and Lynda would encourage partygoers to do something outside their comfort zone like experimenting with color, or perhaps trying a new technique.

Safety First

Be sure your guests know about safety precautions ahead of time. I mixed the dyes prior to their arrival to avoid unintended inhalation of the powder. If the technique you choose for your party requires participants to handle powdered dye, be sure to have proper dust masks available for everyone.

In advance of your guests' arrival, be well informed about the products you are using—read the manufacturers' labels carefully and thoroughly. Use pans, utensils, and other implements that are dedicated to nonfood use.

What to Wear

Remind your guests that fabric dye can cause permanent stains, so old clothes and shoes are best. Dye also stains skin, so I provided disposable plastic gloves to protect hands. Eyeglasses should fit snugly and long hair should be tied back.

Consider providing white aprons as a party favor—they'll be an extra layer of protection during the day and act as an ongoing art project as guests wipe their hands or test a color choice. At the end of the day, they can be dropped into a dye bath for overall color.

The dye concentrate, mixed with water in individual jars, is labeled by color.

Using kitchen twine to wrap a scarf around a piece of PVC pipe for shibori dyeing.

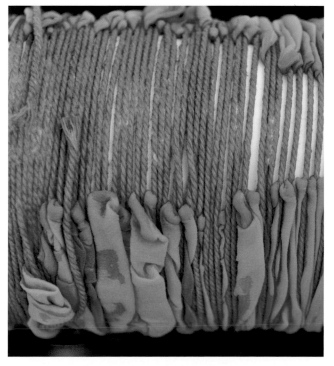

The shibori-wrapped scarf comes out of the dye bath.

BE PREPARED

- Have clean-up cloths available on each table. If you use PFD fabric, these cloths, which are sometimes the best dyed pieces of the day, can have a life after the party.

- Using alphabet beads, string your guests' initials onto a large safety pin and have them ready to attach to the fabric. After the pieces come out of the dye bath, you'll know whose is whose.

- Provide take-away bags filled with a small amount of Synthrapol, an extra set of gloves, and written instructions on rinsing, washing, and drying the hand-dyed fabric.

- Supply plastic bags or containers for safely transporting the freshly dyed fabric home.

- Be sure to dispose of dyes responsibly.

Immersing a shibori-wrapped scarf in the dye bath.

The scarf at left was dyed with the shibori dyeing method, while the scarf at right was dyed with the low-water immersion method.

How to Set Up

I hosted my party outdoors and covered folding tables with heavyweight painter's plastic. As Carol said, "Plan on giving each guest their own table if possible. Dyeing can get your motor going and you need space to spread out."

I positioned the tables near an outdoor faucet and also provided buckets of clean water for rinsing gloves and tools. Large zipper bags and lidded plastic containers were useful at all stages of the party, including the end of the day to hold damp fabric and other freshly dyed items.

Before my guests arrived, I mixed several buckets of soda ash solution, ready for my guests to toss in items they brought with them to dye. I also presoaked the scarves and fabric I provided so folks could get right to work.

Make It fun

Everyone likes to be challenged, and advanced techniques, like shibori, might be best accomplished by pairs of more experienced dyers. One guest can hold the pipe and fabric while the other wraps elastic bands or string around the fabric.

April suggested guests could stamp or stencil onto their washed and dried fabric. Robin mentioned putting rock salt onto the fabric during the dyeing process to get a speckled effect. And there are numerous variations on the Internet for classic tie-dyeing.

Lastly, Carol thought a group project would be fun: Provide a variety of different colored dyes in small squeeze bottles and lay out a piece of PFD fabric large enough to share. Let each guest squirt, drip, dab, and doodle dye onto the fabric. Put it out to dry and cut it into equal parts for each participant. Yet another party favor!

Textiles hang from the tree to dry after dyeing.

EXPERT TIPS

- The hardware store is a great resource for dyers. Five-gallon (19 L) buckets, gloves, mason jars, and painter's plastic are among my favorite items. I especially love the wide-mouthed mason jars because they have marks on the side for measuring, they are easy to clean, and they don't get stained by the dyes.

- A clothesline is a must! Not only is it a practical way to dry fabric, but seeing a line full of pretty colored fabric is extremely gratifying for the participants.

- Pinking shears don't get the credit they deserve. To prevent unraveling of raw-edged fabric in the dyeing process and subsequent washing and drying, cut the pieces of fabric with pinking shears or a wavy-edged rotary blade. You will find this eliminates the mess of thread nests in the dryer.

- Write dyeing notes in permanent marker on a small piece of Tyvek and then staple it to the fabric. The Tyvek will remain undyed and can withstand washing and drying.

LESSONS LEARNED FROM AN ART COLLABORATION

Creating a slice quilt with like-minded artists.

kathy kerstetter

Lunchtime in Bronson Park
10 panels, each 15" × 30" (38 cm × 76 cm)

QUILT PANELS BY
(FROM LEFT TO RIGHT):

Jackie Skarritt, Jenny Grunberg,
Kathy Kerstetter, Ann Berger, Diane Oakes,
Jean DeSavage, Carolyn Zinn, Sheryl Drenth,
Mary Baggerman, and June Belitz.

The Kalamazoo (Michigan) Art Quilt Group is an energetic, creative, and innovative collection of quilt artists. We create monthly, themed challenges and one or more collaborative challenges annually. The largest group challenge to date used a panoramic photo from Bronson Park in the center of downtown Kalamazoo as inspiration. We sliced the photo into ten pieces, with each artist creating a 15" × 30" (38 cm × 76 cm) interpretation of the photo as their slice.

We began this collaborative art piece as something that would be a challenge to each of us, and found we learned more about ourselves, each other, our art, and our community than expected. It has opened up opportunities we never imagined—from an interview on our local National Public Radio station to an exhibit at a nearby hospital.

Many quilt groups are intrigued by the thought of creating similar collaborative art or what is called a "slice quilt." At first glance, it seems like it would be an easy endeavor; in reality there are many things to consider.

Selecting the Image

Look at your photographs carefully before choosing an image to portray in a slice quilt. Not all photographs work well for this type of quilt.

When selecting an image, one of the most important things is to make sure there is one unifying element that ties the slices together, such as a sidewalk, building, shoreline, and so on. Once the collaboration is complete and hung with each artist's unique style, this unifying element will bring the quilt together. In "Lunchtime in Bronson Park," we focused on sidewalk lines to lead the eye from slice to slice.

The second thing to consider in your photo selection is the amount of detail in the scene; too much detail may overwhelm the artists and viewers, while lack of detail could minimize the depth.

Lastly, lines should be drawn on the master photo to determine how it will be divided; look closely at each portion to make sure each member has something interesting to portray in their section.

Choose the Artists

It is easy to get excited about working with your friends on a collaboration; in reality, sometimes even close friends may not be the best choice, depending on your desired outcome. Decide whether the project will be open to anyone who wants to participate or whether it will be invitational.

As you go through the process of selecting artists, consider their previously completed projects and quality of work. Do they complete their projects or set them aside when they hit a glitch? If there is a deadline for a project, do they meet it? Also, think about the quality of the person's work, and imagine what their work might look like in a slice quilt next to other slices.

We included ten participants in our collaboration, which is probably the largest number that should be in a group for it to work smoothly. Most members in our group felt that four to six individuals would be the ideal number for this type of art.

The last but perhaps most important factor to consider in potential participants is their communication skills. As deadlines loom, it is frustrating and stressful if there are one or two members who stop or delay communicating with the rest of the group. Think back to other communications that you have had with these potential members and consider how promptly they are responding to emails and how frequently they attend regular meetings. Members who are not reliable may require additional phone calls and home visits to retrieve information or their artwork—or worse! The most senior member of our group is 83 and she said it best, "If you commit to a group and hand them your email address, you should be checking and responding to email daily."

Create a Smooth Collaboration

The first thing a newly formed group should do is meet to decide how the collaboration will be facilitated.

Consider and Decide Collectively on an Action Plan:

• Choose milestones for the completion of the quilt, such as planning during the first month, patterns made/fabric selected during the second month, and so on.

• Create a plan of action if someone is not meeting deadlines and/or stops communicating with the group.

• Determine what kind of liberties members may take with their slice. Should everything that is in the original image appear on the quilt slice? Can you add things such as flag poles or people to the image? And if you do take liberties with the quilt, should you notify the group?

• Discuss the important match-up points for adjacent slices.

- Choose the method for finishing quilt edges—one-color binding, pieced-binding, a faced edge, or raw edge.

- Decide how disagreements will be resolved; whether you need to come to a consensus or majority vote rules.

- Select one person as leader for the group.

This agreement does not have to be a contract; instead have one person type the guidelines into an email and everyone just needs to reply with "agreed."

Make a Slice of the Quilt

We all make quilts and think about their approximate finished sizes, but in this case you must end up with an exact size because each quilt slice will hang next to one or two slices made by others; the closer everyone is to the exact measurement, the better the collective quilt will look while hanging. Sounds easy, right? It is tougher than it sounds. When creating a slice, extend the work at least 1" (2.5 cm) around all edges; remember, quilting the slice may cause shrinkage.

The method used for the finished edge will also affect the dimensions of the quilt. If you bind the quilt, you will probably extend the measurement each direction by ⅛–½" (3 mm–1.3 cm). If you face the quilt, you could lose the same amount or even more. Make a small mock-up and see how the measurements change when finishing the outer edges.

These are some of the things we learned from our collaboration. Was everything perfect? Smooth? No. Would we do it again? Absolutely!

ADDITIONAL TIPS FOR WORKING TOGETHER

- Determine the reason your group is doing this project (for fun, to challenge the members, for publication, etc).

- Create a recovery plan in case a member cannot complete their slice.

- Document agreed-upon sizes, colors, finishing techniques, and so on, and communicate those decisions clearly to all group members.

- Meet on a regular basis and show progress.

- Identify the preferred communication method for the group (email, Facebook, phone).

MINIATURE PRAYER FLAGS

Creating a meaningful group project.

jenn mason

It is wonderful for a group to celebrate special events or help provide support in sadder times. As creative individuals, we love to give from our hearts using our artistic talents. Getting an entire group together to take on a big creative project can be a challenge—but that doesn't mean they care any less.

This prayer-flags-under-glass project is the perfect solution for time-strapped group giving. Every member can participate whether they work together in the same room or miles away. The pleasure for the participants is not only the joy seen on the recipient's face, but also the stress-free enjoyment of whipping up a tiny part of the greater whole. The mismatched supplies rendered into multiple flag shapes make a cohesive finished project in their joint eccentricity. Skill level is also not a hindrance, as a simple running stitch looks lovely next to a French-knotted wonder.

These flags were made by the staff of Cloth Paper Scissors, Stitch, *and* Quilting Arts *magazines.*

MATERIALS

- Fabric scraps
- Embellishments
- ⅛" (3 mm) wide ribbon
- Shadow box
- Handsewing supplies
- Tracing paper
- Pencil
- Templates

Make a Flag

1. Trace the templates below onto tracing paper and cut them out.

2. Using the templates as your guide, cut out the flag shapes from the fabric scraps. Embellish and decorate the flags to your heart's content.

3. Fold the top of the flags to the back on the dotted line and handstitch close to the raw edge, leaving an opening for the ribbon.

4. Arrange the flags in a pleasing manner and string them on a thin ribbon.

TIPS FOR GROUPS

- Choose a color theme.
- To hang flags in a zigzag fashion, string those that drape right facing frontwards, and those that drape left facing backwards.
- Tie a slipknot to create a loop for the pins holding the flags in place.

This shadow box contains 23 flags made by the staff of Cloth Paper Scissors, Stitch, *and* Quilting Arts *magazines.*

TEMPLATE

Template is printed at actual size.

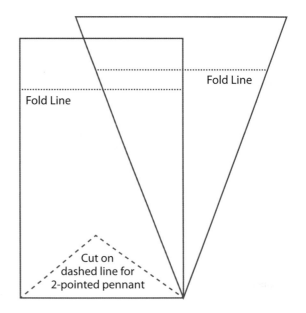

Fold Line

Fold Line

Cut on dashed line for 2-pointed pennant

"

The mismatched supplies
rendered into multiple flag shapes
make a cohesive finished project
in their joint eccentricity.

"

MAKE A VILLAGE

Fabric houses with an art-quilt flair.

jacqueline deRuyter

Do you have tiny scraps, selvedges, and fabric strips sitting around that are too pretty to throw away but too small to use? My pretty piles were building up but I was determined to put them to good use. By layering and quilting the scraps, I ended up with a beautifully textured material with enough firmness to create 3-D structures.

The versatility and pliability of fiber make it an ideal foundation on which to layer techniques. My houses begin with a flat canvas created from many small pieces of fiber that are dyed, painted, and stitched, then cut apart and reassembled. I make houses because they are relatively simple structures and easy to embellish. The ability to add materials as the house evolves is the reason I love the step-by-step construction process. Each house takes on its own personality, and I name each finished house after a place I've lived or visited.

MATERIALS

*Finished Size: 10" × 2½" × 2½"
(25.5 cm × 6.5 cm × 6.5 cm)*

- A variety of thin fabric strips in both light neutrals and black, approximately ¼" × 6" (6 mm × 15 cm) (I used my stash of strips from past projects.)

- Sew-in heavyweight stabilizer, ½ yard (0.5 m) (I used Pellon #50.)

- Polyester stuffing

- Embellishments such as beads, additional fabric, and embroidery thread

- Cotton quilting thread

- Fabric dye (I used RIT Dye.)

- Fabric paints (I used Jacquard Lumiere fabric paint.)

- Quilt basting spray

- Stamps (purchased or handmade)

- Roof template, provided

Make the Walls

1. Cut a 6" × 11" (15 cm × 28 cm) piece of heavyweight stabilizer and spray it with basting spray.

2. Arrange the neutral fabric strips horizontally on the sprayed side of the interfacing. Overlap the strips to prevent the interfacing from showing through (**FIGURE 1**). This piece will become the walls.

3. Quilt it heavily with white cotton quilting thread. I usually quilt in a wavy grid pattern. Free-motion quilting works well, but be sure to stitch very densely (**FIGURE 2**).

4. Prepare a dye bath following the manufacturer's instructions. Submerge the entire piece into the dye. I often create an ombré effect by letting one side of the stitched panel sit in the dye longer than the other. Remove the fabric from the dye bath and rinse and dry it according to the manufacturer's instructions.

5. Once the piece is dry, stamp on designs using fabric paint. Use purchased stamps or look around your house for inspiration. My favorite stamp is the end of an empty spool of thread (**FIGURE 3**).

6. Cut the quilted panel into (4) 2½" × 5" (6.5 cm × 12.5 cm) rectangles.

7. Embellish as desired with beads, topstitching, or more fabric. Make doors and windows with scraps. This is when you can give your house its own personality. Leave ¼" (6 mm) free on the edges of the walls to allow for the assembly.

FIG. 1

FIG. 2

FIG. 3

A FEW WORDS ABOUT DYEING

- Different fabrics accept dye differently. Use this to your advantage to create variation in color by including some noncotton fabric strips.

- Experiment with your dyes. Try painting the dye on with a brush rather than submerging to create different intensities. Or skip the dye and use watercolor paints.

- If you are unhappy with your initial dye result, try overdyeing with the same dye or a different color.

Make the Roof and Base

1. Cut a 6" × 14" (15 cm × 35.5 cm) piece of heavyweight interfacing. Spray it with the basting spray and arrange the black fabric strips on it horizontally.

2. Quilt heavily with black quilting thread.

3. Using the roof template, trace and cut out 4 roof pieces. For the base, cut a 2½" (6.5 cm) square.

| **TIP:** *Save those scraps! The trimmed-off pieces make beautiful embellishments for other projects. Many of the windows and doors on my houses are leftovers from previous projects.*

Complete the House

1. Attach a roof piece to each wall piece using a zigzag stitch (**FIGURE 4**). I use a stitch length of 0.5 mm and a width of 3.5 mm.

2. Assemble the house by attaching the sides of the roof pieces to each other using the same zigzag stitch. It is easier to begin at the base and work toward the peak (**FIGURE 5**).

3. Zigzag the base to the bottom of 1 of the walls. This will make it easier to close the bottom of the house once it is stuffed (**FIGURE 6**).

4. Zigzag the sides together. This process is a bit awkward but the interfacing is quite flexible and will tolerate a bit of folding and bending (**FIGURE 7**).

5. Stuff the house with polyester stuffing, taking care not to overfill. Attach the base piece by hand using a whipstitch.

Now that you've made one, you can imagine the possibilities. The dimensions of your house can easily be altered to achieve a different effect. Some of my favorite houses have very elongated roofs. These houses are so much fun to create, you'll have your own little village in no time!

FIG. 4

FIG. 5

FIG. 6

FIG. 7

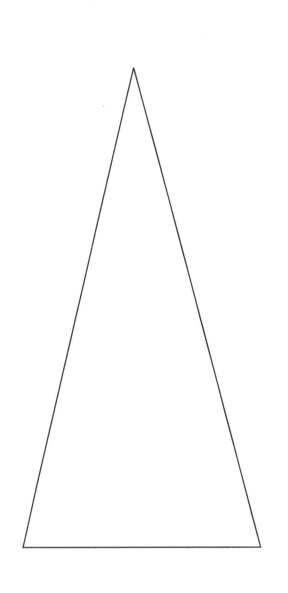

ROOF TEMPLATE

Template is printed at actual size.

Print at 100% with no scaling.

This square should measure 1"
(2.5 cm) when printed.

CHAPTER 6

MAKE IT *now!*

CREATIVE PROJECTS TO SHARE & TRADE

EMBRACING MISTAKES

Tips for nurturing your creative self.

lynn krawczyk

There is a word that is not allowed in my studio: "perfect." I consider it the ultimate creativity killer. It sets up the expectation that if something does not come out just so, then it's not worth doing. Nothing I make is perfect. Ever. There is always something crooked or smudged or maybe even just plain odd. But in all honesty, I wouldn't have it any other way.

The truth is, I've learned far more from my mistakes than from any other teacher. I consider my failures just as sacred and valuable as my successes. This is not to say I'm immune to the frustrations that come when a piece didn't go the way I had hoped. Au contraire. I have a bin (with a lid) that I call the "Time-Out Box." Work that has decided to run amok gets tucked in there until I have the patience to deal with it.

- Fabric frustrations from your Time-Out Box
- Felt or batting scraps
- 3½" × 5" (9 cm × 12.5 cm) pocket sketchbook
- Felt
- Fabric glue
- Chenille needle, size 18
- Perle cotton, size 5
- Rotary cutting supplies

OPTIONAL

- ¾" (2 cm) magnets

Fabric Coaster Mosaic;
at right, Fabric Tile Pocket Sketchbooks.

Creating and Using Time-Out Box

My Time-Out Box serves three main purposes:

Clearing the Decks

Having work that I am unhappy with staring me in the face and hogging up room on my worktable only fuels an environment of frustration. By moving it out of my sight, I'm able to focus on new work instead of dwelling on what I didn't like in the previous piece.

Gaining Distance

Often, what I thought I hated about something doesn't seem quite so bad once I've had some time away. It could just be that I was unhappy with the work because it wasn't what I pictured in my head, not because a technique or color or stitch was off.

Bravery

Putting the work off to the side files it away as a nonpriority. If it's still something I'm not thrilled with when I let it see the light of day again, I'll usually use it for experimentation. I already don't like it so what's the worst that can happen—I'll like it less? It's a free pass to push the boundaries without the worry of "ruining" a good piece.

I know some artists who promptly put work that they have deemed unsuccessful into the trash bin and move on. And if that works for you, then I say go for it. There are no rules regarding work you don't like.

But I'm a pragmatist. I can't get around the idea that I invested time, material, and effort into creating a piece of fabric—and with that comes a fierce determination to figure out ways in which my mistakes can be used.

Plato said, "Necessity is the mother of invention." I doubt he said it in response to artistic angst but it still applies to work that finds its way into the Time-Out Box.

The common element in work that I reinvent is this: Everything looks better when it's smaller. In tinier pieces, shapes and colors are broken down to individual elements. Instead of a large piece that isn't harmonious, you now have isolated little gems of goodness that play well together or on their own. My size of choice is the 1" (2.5 cm) square.

I have three go-to projects for work that emerges from the Time-Out Box. They are functional, quick to make, good for gift giving, and provide a happy home for work I wasn't feeling the love for at first.

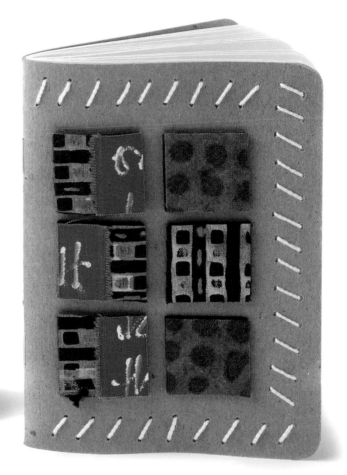

❝ Don't be afraid to reinvent the purpose of artwork that you're not immediately happy with. There is nearly always a gem waiting there to be discovered. ❞

Fabric Tile Pocket Sketchbooks

All of my work is fused to a felt or batting foundation. If your work is not, you will need to add some thickness to the piece before using it in the projects listed below. Fusible batting or interfacing works well.

1. Square up the piece of fabric by trimming 1 edge with a rotary cutter. Create fabric tiles by cutting 1" (2.5 cm) strips, then subcut the strips into 1" (2.5 cm) pieces **(FIGURE 1)**.

| **TIP:** *Cut squares from several different fabrics. It's the mixture of colors and shapes that makes these projects more interesting. Plus, it breaks up work that holds a stigma in your mind as being unsuccessful.*

2. Arrange the fabric tiles in a 4 × 3 grid until you are happy with the pattern **(FIGURE 2)**.

3. With the pocket sketchbook right side up on your work surface, glue the bottom row down first, about ¼" (6 mm) in from the spine edge and bottom of the book. Line the tiles up against each other. Continue adding tiles to make your grid. Just go easy on the glue. Too much glue can warp the journals. You can always add more glue to a loose tile if necessary.

4. After the grid is glued down, add an embellishment fabric tile to the center of the grid **(FIGURE 3)**.

| NOTE: *An embellishment tile is just what it sounds like—a tile with a button or bead sewn to it. It adds a little flair without being overpowering—plus, it's a chance to use up leftover pieces. The embellishment on my book measures 2" × 1½" (5 cm × 3.8 cm).*

5. Using a size 18 chenille needle, poke holes through the cover to create a pattern for hand stitching. Come up from the back for the first stitch and then continue in a running stitch pattern across the holes until you've completed the line of stitching **(FIGURE 4)**.

6. Tie your thread off on the inside of the journal cover by running the needle beneath the next-to-the-last stitch and pull the thread through until it forms a loop **(FIGURE 5)**.

7. Pass the needle through the thread loop and pull through completely so the thread forms a knot.

NOTHING'S PERFECT

If you're like me and a 1" (2.5 cm) square doesn't always measure exactly 1" (2.5 cm), don't stress. Either trim the pieces to be a uniform size or just go with the flow and snug them in next to each other. On the other hand, if you leave them as is, all it means is that the edges of the fabric won't line up exactly, but that little bit of imperfection adds interest.

Additional Projects

After you've made a custom sketchbook, think of other ways to use the fabric tiles and handstitched details in other arrangements. Follow the same steps for cutting the fabric tiles to make button magnets and mosaic coasters. And remember, you can embellish the fabric tiles to your heart's content— beads, trim, more surface design. The sky's the limit!

Button Magnets

Stitch a button to the front of the tile in order to make it more rigid. Apply glue to a ¾" (2 cm) magnet and press the fabric tile in place. You've made an (almost) instant refrigerator or message board magnet.

Fabric Mosaic Coasters

Since I need that extra-large cup of coffee in the morning, I like slightly larger coasters. Cut a 5½" (14 cm) square of felt for the base of each coaster. Starting ⅛" (3 mm) in from the lower left corner, stitch each tile in place with a large cross stitch. Trim the felt evenly around the coaster leaving a small amount of the felt extending beyond the tiles for a touch of color.

FIG. 1

FIG. 2

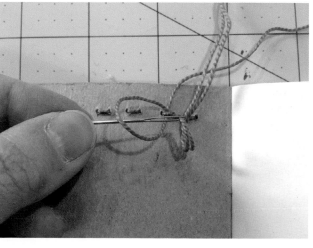

FIG. 3

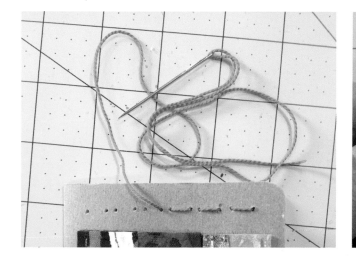

FIG. 4

FIG. 5

CREATE A FRAGMENT FABRIC BOOK

Inspired storytelling with photos and cloth.

lesley riley

Bookmaking with fabric collage is a fun and liberating way to use fabric and ephemera—coupled with your photos and memories—to create something meaningful and lasting. The charm and appeal of these books come from the spontaneous way the pages are created. And once you cut your pages to size, all measuring is over.

Fabric provides an endless variety of color, texture, and pattern. Working in the book form will spark ideas and lead you to a whole new way of looking at your stash. Don't worry if you don't have a large fabric stash, you only need little scraps to make a fragment fabric book.

All of my pages have a photo as the focal point, often one with a face. We will always look at another face before anything else. If you choose to use text on the page, in the form of a word or a quotation, that will be the second thing that will capture the viewer's attention. We're nosy by nature. We want to know what someone else has to say. But a face and a few words will not capture anyone's attention for long. That's where the fabric comes in.

Fabric is a part of our lives from beginning to end and when we create art with fabric, we can live on through our fabric creations. Certain fabrics also have deep connotations for us—think about schoolgirl

MATERIALS

Makes a 10-page 10" × 8" (25.5 cm × 20.5 cm) book; the outside pages will be the front and back cover.

- Transfer paper (I used TAP Transfer Artist Paper.)

- Photos scanned into a computer (Use your own or copyright-free images.)

- Quotes or text scanned or typed into your computer

- White cotton or muslin, fat quarter (18" × 22" [45.5 cm × 56 cm]) or ½ yard (0.5 m) depending on the size and quantity of the items you wish to transfer

- Lightweight fusible web, 20" × 2 yards (51 cm × 1.8 m)

- Midweight fabric for book pages, 6 pieces each 10" × 16" (25.5 cm × 40.5 cm)

  | NOTE: *Fabric pieces should measure twice as long and the same height as the finished page. Suggested fabrics: denim, linen, home décor, ticking*

- Assortment of fabric for page collages in a variety of color, scale, texture, and pattern

- Scissors or rotary cutter and mat

- For hand binding:

- Clothespins or clamps

- Strong sewing needle, 3" (7.5 cm)

- Buttonhole, carpet, or waxed linen thread

- 6 buttons with 2 holes each, ½–1" (1.3–2.5 cm)

OPTIONAL

- Appliqué pressing sheet or parchment paper

plaids, prints and colorways from the 1960s, antique lace collars, or crisp white linen. While I choose my fabrics at random, I always try to create a mood or a memory, or evoke a time or a place. Keep this in mind when you work. Does this fabric remind you of Depression-era wallpaper, a spring garden, or a summer beach? What image would complement the fabric? What fabric would enhance the message in the image you have chosen?

Gather your fabrics and photos, choose a theme or storyline, find some words or quotes to help you tell the story, and let's make a book!

Prepare the Transfers

1. Print your scanned photos, quotes, and words in reverse onto TAP, following the manufacturer's instructions. Cut around each image, leaving a ¼" margin.

| **TIP:** *If your fabric fragment book has a title and/or you wish to create a label, print it on TAP now. Iron it on to the fabric of your choice and set it aside for a later step.*

2. Press the photos, quotes, and words, image side down, onto white cotton or muslin, following the manufacturer's directions. Use an appliqué pressing sheet or parchment paper to protect the iron and ironing surface.

3. Trim the transferred photos and quotes as desired for the collages and set them aside for a later step.

Create the Pages

1. Fold the book page fabrics in half, to 10" × 8" (25.5 cm × 20.5 cm), and finger press the fold to set a crease. Set aside 2 pieces of fabric—1 for the outer cover and 1 for the inside lining—for a later step.

| NOTE: *The interior pages will be fused back to back and then stacked on top of each other to create the book. To determine how the pages will relate to each other, make a little paper model to show which pages will face each other when the pages are stacked and folded.*

2. Working with the remaining book page fabrics, open 1 piece of fabric. Gather the fused and trimmed transfers and the assortment of fabric (which is unfused). Working on the left "page" of the fabric, create a collage. Repeat on the right "page" with another collage. Repeat some fabrics throughout the book to create unity, harmony, and a common look.

3. Tuck bits of fusible web under the fabric pieces. Press the collage in place.

4. Add hand- and/or machine stitching now, if desired. Make 4 spreads.

5. Fuse 2 collaged spreads, wrong sides together. Repeat with the other 2 collaged spreads.

6. Add a title to the cover, if desired. Fuse the cover and inside lining, wrong sides together. Add the label, if using. Stack the other fused folios on top of the lined cover, with the lining facing up. Fold the spreads in half to see how the book will look.

| NOTE: *Adding more pages will make the book thicker and the cover should be cut a bit longer to accommodate the extra depth.*

7. Unfold the spreads and pin the layers together.

DEFINITIONS

FOLIO: A sheet of paper folded in half, creating two leaves (which is the equivalent of four pages).

SIGNATURE: A group of folios that are folded and stitched together.

SPREAD: Two facing pages in a book.

Finish the Book

Bind your book by machine or by hand.

By Machine

1. Insert bobbin thread in your sewing machine that coordinates with your cover pages. The bobbin thread will be visible down the spine on the outside of the book.

2. Machine stitch down the center to bind the book.

By Hand with a Button Binding

1. Secure the spreads together with clothespins or clamps, with the book's center pages facing up.

2. From the center spread, stick a sturdy straight pin through the center of the signature and out through the spine. Wiggle it a little to create a slight channel for the needle and thread to go through. Repeat 1" (2.5 cm) from the top of the spread and 1" (2.5 cm) from the bottom. Mark the location of the holes, front and back, with a pencil. Remove the pin when you're ready to stitch.

3. Thread the needle and have the buttons handy. Leaving a 3" (7.5 cm) tail of thread and aiming toward the pencil dot on the spine, make a stitch through all of the pages. Pull the thread through the layers and through 1 of the holes in the button. Put the needle through the other hole and back through the spine. Repeat to secure the button. Tie off the thread tails on the inside of the book and knot securely. Repeat with the remaining 2 buttons.

BE LIBERATED

I try never to plan a page ahead of time. Let unexpected combinations in color, pattern, and scale occur.

While I say that I break the rules, these are the three design principles that I do employ religiously—proportion, balance, and variety. You can get almost any fabrics to work together by using these three principles. The secret is in how much of each fabric to use. Sometimes just a sliver of an unexpected color or pattern can make the whole page sing.

JEWELS FOR THE WALL

Framing whimsical window-inspired quiltlets.

natalya aikens

You know all those fabulous little scraps you just can't bear to part with—the trimmed edges of your big art quilts, the little experimental pieces that tug at your heart, and the leftover bits of a fabulous hand-dye that are filling up that basket in your studio? There is a life for them beyond your loving gaze!

Take these little jewels out of the basket, spread them out on your worktable, and play! Then put them into a frame and embellish.

I like to arrange the scraps in a simple composition, reminiscent of a window. Windows have always held my imagination and I use them frequently in my art quilts. So it was a natural transition to make fun little window quiltlets. And the leap to frame and embellish them? Well you can imagine how easy that was!

MATERIALS

- Fabric and quilt scraps
- Small wooden frame
- Heavyweight interfacing (I used Pellon 70 Peltex.)
- Fusible web, small pieces
- 3-D paints (I used Ranger Liquid Pearls, Duncan Scribbles 3D, and Jacquard Lumiere 3D.)
- Acrylic paint
- Fine grade sandpaper
- Fine-tip permanent markers (I used Sharpie Oil-Based Paint Markers and Sakura Gelly Roll pens.)
- Paintbrushes, variety of sizes

FIND YOUR OWN WINDOW INSPIRATION

Because I enjoy using my Russian heritage as inspiration for my art, I used traditional Russian village windows as my jumping off point. I looked through reference books, my own photos, and even took an Internet tour to gather my inspiration. I printed a few images for a visual reference as I worked. You can do the same with your inspiration, be it a window, a landscape, or a still life.

Make the Jeweled Quiltlet

1. Take the glass out of the frame. Trace it on the heavy interfacing. Mark the center for a visual reference. Add approximately 1" (2.5 cm) on all sides and cut out the interfacing.

2. Trace the glass on the fusible web. Cut out the fusible web and center it on the interfacing.

3. Dig into your scraps! Play with different textures and colors until you find a pleasing combination that resembles a window shape. Sometimes these come together quickly and other times it takes some digging to come up with the right choices. Once you have the pieces for your window, arrange them on the fusible web and fuse in place, following manufacturer's instructions.

4. Evaluate your composition. Is it complete or does it need more detail? Add a few more scraps on top of the initial shape, if necessary. I usually have a sliver of a heavily stitched piece that just begs to become a tiny detail. Pin that piece into place or use a bit of fusible to adhere it to your quiltlet.

5. Choose a thread that matches, coordinates, or contrasts with your fabrics. Have fun with your choice. I usually pick a variegated or a multicolored thread because I love the sketchy qualities they add to my quiltlets. Use free-motion stitching to outline the window shape and go over your stitched line multiple times to create a thick line and secure the edges.

6. Once you have the basic outline, add curls, swirls, and circles if you wish. Use your artist's eye to decide if this little jewel needs that extra stitching. Once you're done with machine stitching, press the piece one last time. (For textural pieces, you may want to skip the pressing.)

7. With a rotary cutter, trim the quiltlet to size using the glass from the frame as a template.

Embellish the Frame

To add to the charm, make each frame different—designed to interact with its own little quiltlet.

1. Prepare the frame for embellishment. If you want to change the color of the frame, lightly sand the wood, wipe off the dust, then paint it with an acrylic paint. Let the paint dry. If you don't want to change the base color of the frame, then don't do a thing and move on to the next step.

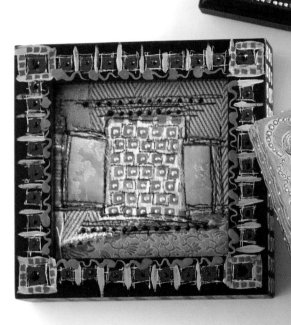

2. When I'm happy with the frame color, I put the quiltlet into the frame. It helps to see the whole picture as I first plan the frame decoration. (See sidebar at left for Natalya's embellishment ideas.)

3. As you embellish the frame, use a variety of thin and thick brushes to paint lines and swirls with acrylic paints in different colors. You can also use a variety of pens and markers to draw lines or swirls directly on the frame. As I know you can't make just one of these jewels, take this opportunity to play and experiment with a different treatment on each different frame until you decide which you prefer. Though you might discover (as I did) that you like them all!

4. For the final touch, I like to add some dimensional effects—it's that final bit of glamour that makes it a jewel. Just a few dots of well-placed 3-D paint will do the job, or you might choose to bedazzle the whole frame. Do what makes you happy! How much of your scrap stash can you use up this way? Only time will tell....

NATALYA'S IDEAS FOR FRAME EMBELLISHMENT

There are infinite ways to decorate each frame, but I'll share my method. Take your cue from your quiltlet and ask these questions:

*   Do you want to extend the stitched lines into the frame?

*   What patterns in the fabric could be echoed?

*   Should you keep going with the curls and swirls and circles that were sketched with thread?

Use these and other questions to help you decide on your embellishment plan.

LITTLE BIRD, LITTLE BIRD

Tiny treasures to keep or gift.

valerie komkov hill

Everyone needs a bit of "charming" now and again, and these adorable tiny art quilts that can do double-duty as decorations or gift tags do the trick. With a piece of original artwork, a few readily available art supplies, and a variety of embellishments, you can create your own version of these lovely designs and tailor them for any occasion.

Tiny art quilts—such as the ones created in this project—have a life of their own. Use them as gift tags, bookmarks, holiday ornaments, or embellishments for larger works. The only limit is your imagination!

MATERIALS

- Original painted image or a digitally altered, copyright-free image

- Scraps of fabric, batting, and interfacing

- Jacquard ExtravOrganza, inkjet printable semi-transparent silk sheets

- Embroidery thread, beads, sequins, and other embellishments

- Silk ribbon or cord for hanging

- Acrylic metallic paint (I used Golden copper and silver.)

- Photo editing software, such as Photoshop or Waterlogue

- Small paintbrush

Make a Tiny Treasure

1. Select a simple image that reads well at a small size. I began with a watercolor of a sparrow cropped from a larger work I painted last year. Choose a subject that interests you, from birds and flowers to bees and leaves.

2. Scan the image into your computer. Open the image with photo editing software and use the effects tools to alter the image to your liking.

| NOTE: *If you choose to use a photograph (either your own or a copyright-free photo) it can be manipulated to look like a painting. Edit the photograph to give the image a softer, more distinctive look. Check out apps for your smartphone that can transform a photo into a watercolor in seconds.*

3. Set your printer to wallet size (2½" × 3¼" [6.5 cm × 8.5 cm]) and print out multiples on a sheet of ExtravOrganza (**FIGURE 1**). Cut the images apart.

4. Cut out a series of 4" × 6" (10 cm × 15 cm) background fabrics. The extra fabric allows you to shift the printed image. Layer the printed images over the fabric as desired (**FIGURE 2**).

| **TIP:** *Fabric that is too busy will overwhelm your printed image. The best fabrics to use are warm-toned prints with open spaces between the patterns.*

5. Make a quilt sandwich of the printed image, the background fabric, a piece of thin, stiff batting or heavy interfacing, and a backing fabric.

| NOTE: *The backing fabric can be any leftover scraps or muslin since it will eventually be covered in a final fabric.*

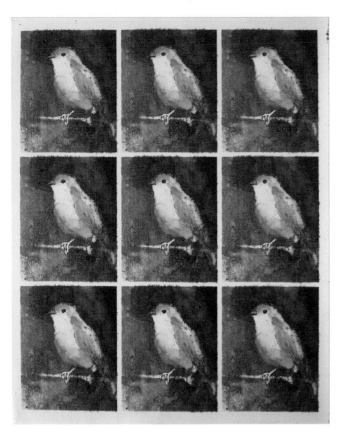

FIG. 1

FIG. 2

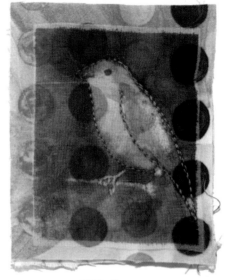

FIG. 3

6. Machine stitch around the image with either a contrasting or matching thread, depending on how much you want the image to pop **(FIGURE 3)**.

7. The tag can now be embellished as desired, adding more machine stitching, embroidery accents, beading, and sequins. Don't worry about knots of thread at the back, as they will be covered **(FIGURE 4)**.

8. Select a final backing fabric and layer the finished quilt on top of it. Stitch an outline all the way around the tag and trim away the excess fabric.

9. Zigzag around the edges of the tag. A loose zigzag will look more rustic or shabby chic, while a tight zigzag or satin stitch will give the tag a more polished look.

10. Use Golden metallic paint and a small flat paintbrush to gently brush the edges of the tag all the way around. This adds some sparkle and also helps seal frayed threads.

11. Sew a silk ribbon loop to the back of the tag for hanging.

| NOTE: *This technique can be used with larger images to create artistic covers for cell phones, tablets, laptops, and eReader cases.*

FIG. 4

Process photos by Valerie Kornkov Hill

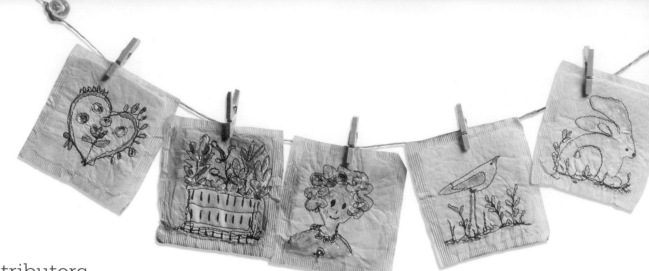

Contributors

NATALYA AIKENS is an artist whose work is deeply rooted in her heritage. She mixes Russian decorative traditions with the elegant architecture of St. Petersburg. Focusing on recycled elements, she uses vintage fabrics, intense hand stitching, free-motion stitching, computer manipulation, and the sketched line to create her pieces. **artbynatalya.com**

JEANNE AIRD is a full-time art teacher living in Paso Robles, California, who enjoys creating and showing her unique art fabric and quilts. Jeanne works with a variety of surface design techniques to create complex layers of pattern on cloth. Most of her quilts are abstract or nature-inspired. **jeanneairdartfabricandquilts.blogspot.com**

SUE BLEIWEISS is a full-time fiber artist living in Massachusetts. Using her own hand-dyed cotton, she creates vibrant, colorful art quilts intended to delight the viewer and make them smile. Sue has appeared on *Quilting Arts TV* and has a Quilting Arts Workshop™ video. She is the author of *Fusible Fabric Collage*. **suebleiweiss.com**

SUSAN BRUBAKER KNAPP is the host of *Quilting Arts TV*. She is a studio fiber artist, author, and teacher and has several Quilting Arts Workshop™ videos. Susan lives near Charlotte, North Carolina, with her husband and two daughters. She teaches both nationally and internationally. **bluemoonriver.com**

TRACI BUNKERS is the author of The Art Journal Workshop and Print & Stamp Lab. She is a more-than-full-time artist who loves repurposing items into printing tools and is happiest when she's getting her art on. **TraciBunkers.com**

ANA BUZZALINO is a fiber artist and quilt instructor living in Calgary, Alberta, Canada. Ana has been teaching quilting techniques for over 25 years. Her recent work focuses on surface design, such as fabric dyeing, rubbings, stampings, and monoprinting. She is a frequent contributor to *Quilting Arts*, has appeared on *Quilting Arts TV*, and has two *Quilting Arts* videos. **anabuzzalino.com**

JANE DAVILA is a fiber artist, media mixer, and collector of found objects. She is the author of *Surface Design Essentials* and the co-author of Art Quilt Workbook and Art Quilts at Play. Jane lives in Ridgefield, Connecticut, with her husband Carlos, an oil painter and sculptor. **JaneDavila.com**

JACQUELINE DERUYTER is a fiber artist happily ling on Cape Cod in Massachusetts. Her work combines traditional quilting techniques with improvisational assembly to create fiber-based sculptures. When not in her studio she can be found enjoying the beauty of the Cape with her husband and three children. **jackiederuyter.com**

ROBIN FERRIER is known for her nonrepresentational and colorful art quilts. Her compositions are organic, original, and use a wide spectrum of colorful fabrics that she dyes herself. Raised in Hawaii, she is influenced by the intense sunlight and natural beauty of her surroundings. Robin enjoys documenting her work on her website and blog. **simplyrobin.com**

JO FITSELL is one of the founders of the Front Range Contemporary Quilters group in Colorado. She teaches fiber art, collage, and creativity classes at the Art Students League in Denver and spends her summers in Ontario, Canada. She exhibits her work in both countries. **jofitsell.com**

LYNDA HEINES is a surface-design artist living in Newburgh, Indiana. She spends most of her free time adding dye and paint to fabric, and sharing her art-making journey through her blog and local classes. **bloombakecreate.com**

KATHY KERSTETTER left corporate America to spend more time in her studio. She teaches at a local community college and spends as much time as possible creating with mixed media. Kathy and her husband, Mark, live in Kalamazoo, Michigan. **kathykerstetter.com**

VALERIE KOMKOV HILL retired after a successful career as a dance instructor and began teaching yoga and devoting her free time to creating art. She works in many media but primarily focuses on acrylic painting and fiber arts. She is an award-winning artist, a member of Studio Art Quilt Associates (SAQA), and a founding member of the Caprock Art Quilters, a SAQA Circle regional affiliate. Valerie's work is often featured in local galleries and art shows.

MARGARITA KORIOTH is a fiber artist and quilt instructor living in Tennessee. She likes to work with a combination of paper and fabric or fabric alone. Her recent work emphasizes surface design such as dyeing, stamping, and silk screening with a focus on lettering on fabric. **margascrafts.blogspot.com**

LYNN KRAWCZYK is a surface-design artist from Plymouth, Michigan. She has written for *Quilting Arts* and *Cloth Paper Scissors* magazines, appeared on *Quilting Arts TV*, and has three Quilting Arts Workshop™ videos: "Print Design Compose," "Color Theory Made Easy," and "Thermofax Screen Printing Essentials." Lynn is the author of *International Printing: Simple Techniques for Inspired Fabric Art* and *The Handstitched Surface*. **smudgeddesignstudio.com**

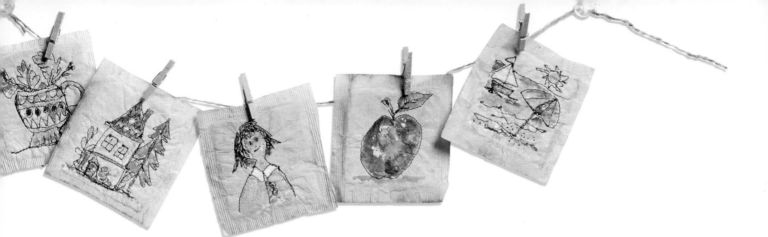

JANE LAFAZIO is a full-time artist with a wide range of skills as a painter, mixed-media and quilt artist, art teacher, and blogger. She teaches drawing and watercolor workshops online and at art retreats internationally. Her artwork has been featured in *Cloth Paper Scissors* and *Quilting Arts* magazines and several books. Jane is a frequent guest on *Quilting Arts TV*. She has several Quilting Arts Workshop™ and Cloth Paper Scissors Workshop™ videos. **janelafazio.com**

KRISTINE LUNDBLAD is an avid quilter and Associate Editor of *Modern Patchwork* magazine. **quiltingcompany.com**

JENN MASON is a former editor of *Cloth Paper Scissors* magazine. In her free time she likes to paint, stitch, collage, and live each day as creatively as possible from her 1870s carriage-house home and studio. **twitter.com/mixedmediajenn**

LORIE MCCOWN has made art all her life—mainly in drawing, painting, paper, textile, and fiber—and infuses her work with spiritual and biblical meanings. Her pieces are in private collections and public galleries nationally and internationally. Lorie's work has been juried into local, national, and international shows and featured in numerous magazines. She teaches workshops and classes nationally in painting, mixed-media, and fiber arts, and has appeared on *Quilting Arts TV*. **loriemccown.com**

JEANNIE PALMER MOORE is a mixed-media fiber artist who is constantly experimenting on fabric with dyes, paints, and just about anything. As a Juried Artist SAQA member, she currently has several quilts traveling the world. She lives in San Diego, California with her husband and German Shorthaired Pointer. **jpmartist.com**

LESLEY RILEY is an internationally known artist, art quilter, teacher, author, developer of Transfer Artist Paper (TAP) and the Artist Success coach, and artist enabler who turned her initial passion for photos, color, and the written word into a dream occupation. **lesleyriley.com**

RITA SUMMERS likes to push boundaries in her art to create her own original style. With a background in contemporary art/craft/design, Rita has chosen stitch as her favorite medium. She often incorporates upcycled materials, found objects, and a mix of artistic processes such as photography, printmaking, collage, sculpture, painting, drawing, and text in her artwork. **gonerustic.wordpress.com**

BERYL TAYLOR grew up in England and moved to the United States with her family in 2002. She qualified in the City & Guilds Creative Embroidery program, is the author of *Mixed-Media*

Explorations and has appeared on *Quilting Arts TV*. She has two Quilting Arts Workshop™ videos, "Layer by Layer" and "Mixed-Media Art Quilts." **beryltaylor.com**

MELANIE TESTA is an accomplished textile and quilt artist. She holds a degree from the Fashion Institute of Technology in Textile/Surface Design and exhibits her fiber art at various galleries and quilt shows around the country. She is an author and fabric designer. **melanietesta.com**

LESLIE TUCKER JENISON is a contemporary quilt maker and fabric designer from San Antonio, Texas. Her award-winning quilts have been juried into national and international exhibitions. In addition to writing and making art, Leslie teaches a variety of workshops and is one half of the Dinner at Eight Artists curating team. **leslietuckerjenison.com**

LAURA WASILOWSKI is a contemporary quilt maker whose artwork is collected and exhibited internationally. Owner of the dye shop Artfabrik, Laura is also a lecturer, quilt instructor, pattern designer, and author. Laura has a Quilting Arts Workshop™ video, "Improvisational Fused Quilt Art" with co-creator Frieda Anderson, and has appeared on *Quilting Arts TV*. **artfabrik.com**

LIBBY WILLIAMSON is a mixed-media fiber artist, quilter, surface designer, painter, and dabbler of most art forms. She uses her sewing machine as a drawing tool with free-motion stitching as her main design elements, enhancing her handpainted fabrics and papers. Libby teaches from her studio in Orange, California, online, and at destination retreats. **libbywilliamsondesigns.blogspot.com**

Metric Conversion Chart

TO CONVERT	TO	MULTIPLY BY
Inches	Centimeters	2.54
Centimeters	Inches	0.4
Feet	Centimeters	30.5
Centimeters	Feet	0.03
Yards	Meters	0.9
Meters	Yards	1.1

MORE INSPIRING BOOKS
for Makers

COLORING WITH THREAD

Stitching a Whimsical World
with Hand Embroidery

Tula Pink

978-1-4402-4811-5

$21.99

MODERN MACHINE QUILTING

Make a perfectly finished quilt
on your home machine

Catherine Redford

978-1-4402-4631-9

$24.99

AVAILABLE AT
YOUR FAVORITE RETAILER OR
QUILTINGCOMPANY.COM